Smart Money: A Teen's Guide to Uı Mastering Finances

CW01500406

Author: Karl Hartey

Hartey Wealth Management Ltd
Hilliards Court
Chester Business Park
Chester
CH4 9QP

First Published 2024

ISBN: 9798344992471

Printed in United Kingdom

All figures correct at time of publication – 02.10.24. Figures may change following future budgets.

Contents

Foreword

Dear Reader,

Welcome to a journey that will help you unlock the mysteries of money and set you on a path to financial success. Whether you're saving for something special, starting your first job, or just curious about how money works, this book is here to guide you through the essentials of managing your finances.

We live in a world where money touches almost every part of our lives. From buying your favourite snacks to thinking about your future career, understanding money is a skill that will help you now and throughout your life. This book is designed specifically for you - young people aged 12 to 16 - who are beginning to make important decisions about money. It's written in a way that's easy to understand, with real-life examples and simple explanations to help you grasp each concept.

Each chapter covers a different aspect of money, from what it is and how it's earned, to more complex topics like taxes, credit cards, and even mortgages. But don't worry, we've broken down everything into manageable pieces so that you can learn at your own pace. Plus, at the end of each chapter, you'll find multiple-choice questions to test your knowledge and make sure you've got the hang of things.

We believe that learning about money early on can make a big difference in your life. It can help you avoid common financial mistakes, plan for your future, and even reach your dreams - whether that's buying your first car, going to university, or starting your own business.

So dive in, take your time, and enjoy the journey. The knowledge you gain here will empower you to take control of your finances and set you on a path to a bright and successful future.

Happy learning!

Karl Hartey

Introduction
for
Teachers and Parents

Dear Teachers and Parents

Welcome to **"Smart Money: A Teen's Guide to Understanding and Mastering Finances."** This book is more than just a guide for young readers - it's a tool designed to empower teens with the knowledge and skills they need to navigate the complex world of money. As a teacher or parent, you play a crucial role in helping your students or children understand the importance of financial literacy and in guiding them through the lessons this book offers.

How to Use This Book:

1. **Start with Open Conversations:** Begin by discussing the importance of money management in daily life. Encourage your students or children to share what they already know about money and what they hope to learn. This will help set the stage for engaged learning.

2. **Set Learning Goals:** Work with your students or children to set clear learning objectives for each chapter. Whether it's understanding how to create a budget, grasping the basics of investing, or learning about taxes, having goals will help them focus on key concepts.

3. **Interactive Learning:** Each chapter in this book includes multiple-choice questions designed to reinforce learning. Encourage your students or children to answer these questions independently and then review their answers together. This can spark discussions and clarify any misunderstandings.

4. **Real-Life Application:** Bring the lessons in the book to life by relating them to real-world situations. Discuss everyday financial decisions like budgeting for a school trip, saving for a new gadget, or understanding how a bank account works. This practical application will make the concepts more relatable and memorable.

5. **Encourage Critical Thinking:** Financial literacy isn't just about understanding money; it's about making informed decisions. Encourage your students or children to think critically about the choices they might face in the future, such as managing a credit card or planning for university expenses.

6. **Use Additional Activities:** Consider supplementing the book with additional activities like budgeting exercises, role-playing scenarios, or even simple financial games. These activities can make learning about money more engaging and fun.

7. **Promote Long-Term Learning:** Financial education is a lifelong journey. Encourage your students or children to continue learning about money management beyond this book. Discuss current events related to finance, explore additional resources, and help them develop a mindset of financial responsibility.

Your Role as a Guide:

As you guide your students or children through "**Smart Money**", your support and encouragement will be invaluable. Be patient, answer questions, and provide reassurance as they navigate through concepts that might be new or challenging. Remember, the goal is to equip them with the confidence and skills to make smart financial decisions now and in the future.

Thank you for partnering in this important journey toward financial literacy. Together, we can help the next generation build a strong foundation for financial success.

Sincerely, Karl Hartey

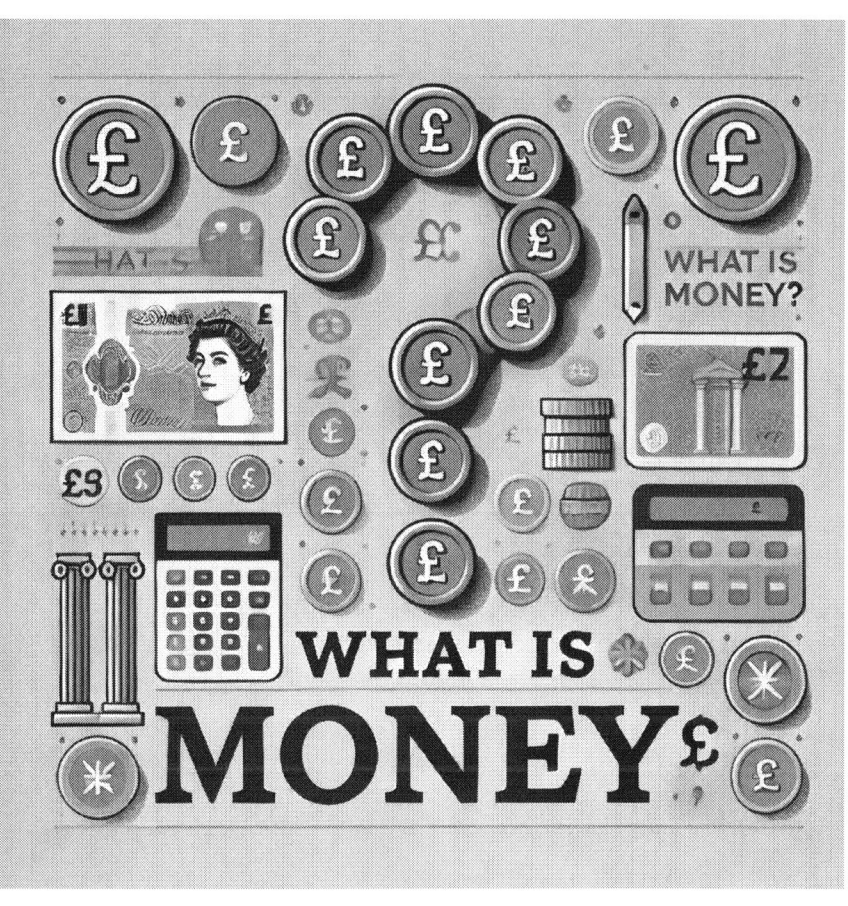

Chapter 1

What is Money?

Introduction: Money is something that we use every day, whether we realise it or not. From buying a snack after school to saving for something special like a new gadget or even a car, money plays a key role in almost everything we do. But have you ever stopped to think: what exactly is money, and why do we rely on it so much? Without understanding money, it can be difficult to make informed choices about earning, saving, or spending. To start mastering the world of finances, it's important to dive deep into the concept of money itself.

What is Money? At its most basic level, money is a tool that makes trading goods and services easier. Imagine a world where there was no money. If you wanted to buy a pair of shoes, you would need to offer something in return - maybe a book or a toy. But what if the shoe seller didn't want your book or toy? This problem, known as the "double coincidence of wants," made bartering difficult. That's where money comes in.

Money serves three key functions:

1. **Medium of Exchange**: Money is something that everyone accepts for goods and services. This makes it much easier to buy things because you don't have to find someone who wants what you're offering.

2. **Store of Value**: Unlike perishable goods like fruits or vegetables, money can be saved and used later without losing its value. This means you can save your money today and use it next month or even next year, and it will still be worth the same (barring inflation).

3. **Unit of Account**: Money provides a standard way to measure and compare the value of different things. For example, when you know that a chocolate bar costs £1 and a T-shirt costs £10, you can easily compare their value.

The History of Money: Before money existed, people used the barter system to trade goods and services. However, bartering had its limitations - it relied on both parties wanting what the other had to offer. For example, if you had vegetables and wanted shoes, you'd have to find someone who had shoes and needed vegetables at that very moment. As you can imagine, this system was complicated and inefficient.

Over time, people began to use items like shells, stones, and metals as a more convenient form of money. These items were easier to trade because they were more widely accepted and held their value. Eventually, people started using metals like gold, silver, and copper to create coins. These metals were valuable, durable, and easy to carry, which made them perfect for use as money.

Paper Money: As societies became more advanced, carrying large quantities of metal coins became impractical. To solve this problem, paper money was introduced. Originally, paper money represented a promise that it could be exchanged for a specific amount of gold or silver. This allowed people to carry lightweight paper instead of heavy coins.

Digital Money: Fast forward to today, and most money isn't physical like coins or paper bills. Instead, much of the money in circulation exists digitally, as numbers in a bank account or balances on a credit card. Digital money is convenient and easy to transfer, making it the preferred form of currency for most transactions today. Even so, it serves the same basic functions as the money of the past.

Different Types of Money:

1. **Cash**: Physical money, such as coins and banknotes, is what most people think of first when they hear the word "money." Cash can be used in everyday transactions, from buying a sandwich to paying for a bus ticket.

2. **Bank Money**: This refers to the money that you keep in a bank account. You can access it through a debit card, cheques, or bank transfers. It's the most common way people manage their money today, especially as we move towards a more cashless society.

3. **Credit Money**: This type of money represents borrowed funds. When you use a credit card or take out a loan, you're spending money that you promise to repay later. Credit money can be very

useful, but it also comes with responsibilities - like paying back what you owe on time.

4. **Cryptocurrency**: This is a new form of digital money, such as Bitcoin or Ethereum. Unlike traditional money issued by governments, cryptocurrencies exist only online and are secured by technology called blockchain. Cryptocurrencies are growing in popularity, but they can be very volatile, meaning their value can change quickly and unpredictably.

Why Money Matters: Understanding money is important because it affects nearly every aspect of our lives. How we earn, spend, save, and invest money determines not only our present-day financial health but also our future. When you know how money works, you're in a better position to make smart choices about how to use it. Whether it's deciding how much to spend, how much to save, or when to invest, having a solid understanding of money can help you avoid debt and reach your financial goals more quickly.

By learning to manage money now, you're setting yourself up for financial independence in the future. Money gives you the freedom to make decisions, whether it's choosing your career path, buying something you really want, or travelling the world. Mastering money isn't just about getting rich; it's about using it wisely to create the life you want.

Multiple Choice Questions:

1. **What is money primarily used for?**

    A) Trading goods and services

    B) Making friends

    C) Creating art

    D) None of the above

2. **What is one key function of money as a "store of value"?**

    A) It helps you store goods for trading

    B) You can save money and use it later without losing its value

    C) It makes money worth more over time

    D) It only applies to physical money like coins

3. **What system did people use before money was invented?**

    A) Credit system

    B) Digital banking

    C) Barter system

    D) Cryptocurrency

4. **Which of the following is an example of credit money?**

   A) Coins

   B) A debit card transaction

   C) A loan from a bank

   D) A cryptocurrency wallet

5. **What was the purpose of introducing paper money?**

   A) To make money look nicer

   B) To avoid carrying heavy metal coins

   C) To trade faster

   D) To prevent theft

6. **Which type of money exists only online and is secured by blockchain technology?**

   A) Bank money

   B) Credit card balance

   C) Cash

   D) Cryptocurrency

Chapter 2

How Money is Earned

Introduction: Money doesn't just appear in your pocket or bank account - you have to earn it. Earning money is a fundamental part of life, and there are many different ways to do it. From working part-time jobs as a teenager to building a full-time career as an adult, understanding how money is earned is the first step towards managing it wisely. This chapter will explore the various ways people earn money, how to recognise the value of work, and the importance of developing skills that can lead to future earning potential.

Ways to Earn Money:

1. **Jobs and Employment**: The most common way people earn money is by working at a job. Jobs can vary widely in terms of hours, tasks, and pay. Some people work part-time, while others have full-time careers. When you work for someone else, you are known as an employee, and the money you receive for your work is called a wage or a salary.

   - **Wages**: Wages are typically paid on an hourly basis. For example, if you work 10 hours a week at £10 per hour, you will earn £100 for that week. Jobs that pay wages often include part-time roles like working in a retail store, café, or doing odd jobs such as babysitting or mowing lawns.

- o **Salaries**: Salaries are fixed amounts paid on a regular basis, often monthly or yearly, regardless of the number of hours you work. For instance, if you earn a salary of £25,000 a year, that amount is divided into monthly payments. Salaries are usually associated with full-time positions like teachers, doctors, and engineers.

2. **Self-Employment**: Not everyone works for someone else. Some people choose to be their own bosses, working as self-employed individuals. If you run your own business, whether it's offering a service like landscaping or selling homemade products online, you are considered self-employed. Being self-employed offers flexibility and the potential to earn more money, but it also comes with added responsibilities, such as managing your own business expenses and taxes.

3. **Freelancing**: Freelancing is similar to self-employment, but it typically involves working on short-term projects for various clients. Freelancers are often hired for their specific skills, such as graphic design, photography, or writing. Instead of working for one employer, freelancers often work for multiple clients and get paid per project. Freelancing offers the freedom

to choose when and where you work, but it can also be unpredictable in terms of income.

4. **Odd Jobs and Part-Time Work**: As a teenager, one of the easiest ways to start earning money is through part-time work or odd jobs. Many teens find work babysitting, dog walking, delivering newspapers, or helping neighbours with outdoor work. Part-time jobs not only help you earn money but also teach important skills like responsibility, time management, and customer service.

5. **Passive Income**: While most income is earned by actively working, some people earn money through passive income. This is money earned from investments, property rental, or royalties from creative works like books or music. Passive income doesn't require constant effort once it's set up, but it often requires a lot of work or investment upfront. For example, if you write a book, you might earn royalties every time a copy is sold, even after the work of writing is done.

The Importance of Skills: Your ability to earn money often depends on the skills you develop. For example, learning how to communicate effectively, manage time, or develop technical expertise can all increase your earning potential. As you grow older, acquiring skills through education, training, or hands-on experience will make it easier to find higher-paying jobs or advance in your chosen career.

The Role of Technology in Earning Money: Technology has changed the way people earn money. Today, many jobs can be done remotely from a computer, and new opportunities have emerged thanks to the internet. Freelancers can find work online, and platforms like YouTube, Etsy, and Twitch allow people to earn money by sharing their content or selling handmade goods. Additionally, social media influencers and content creators can earn money through advertising, brand partnerships, and sponsorships.

Why It's Important to Earn Money: Earning money gives you independence and the freedom to make choices about how you spend, save, and invest. It helps you provide for your basic needs, but it also allows you to pursue your goals and dreams. Whether you're saving for something small, like a new game, or something big, like university or your first car, the money you earn will play a vital role in making it happen.

Multiple Choice Questions:

1. **What is the main difference between wages and salaries?**

    A) Wages are paid yearly, while salaries are paid hourly

    B) Salaries are fixed amounts, while wages are based on the hours worked

    C) Wages are only earned from self-employment

    D) Salaries are only paid to freelancers

2. **What does it mean to be self-employed?**

    A) You work for multiple companies at once

    B) You work for a company that gives you flexible hours

    C) You run your own business and are responsible for managing your income

    D) You work part-time for an employer

3. **Which of the following is an example of passive income?**

    A) Working a retail job

    B) Earning money from investments or property rentals

    C) Freelancing as a photographer

    D) Babysitting for neighbours

4. **How do freelancers typically earn money?**

    A) They work for one employer full-time

    B) They are paid on a yearly salary

    C) They work on short-term projects for multiple clients

    D) They are paid only in commissions

5. **Why are skills important when it comes to earning money?**

    A) Skills determine how much you need to spend each month

    B) Skills increase your ability to earn more money and advance in your career

    C) Skills help you avoid taxes

    D) Skills are only important in self-employment

6. **How has technology changed the way people earn money?**

   A) It has made most traditional jobs obsolete

   B) It allows people to earn money online and work remotely

   C) It has eliminated the need for freelancing

   D) It has made self-employment impossible

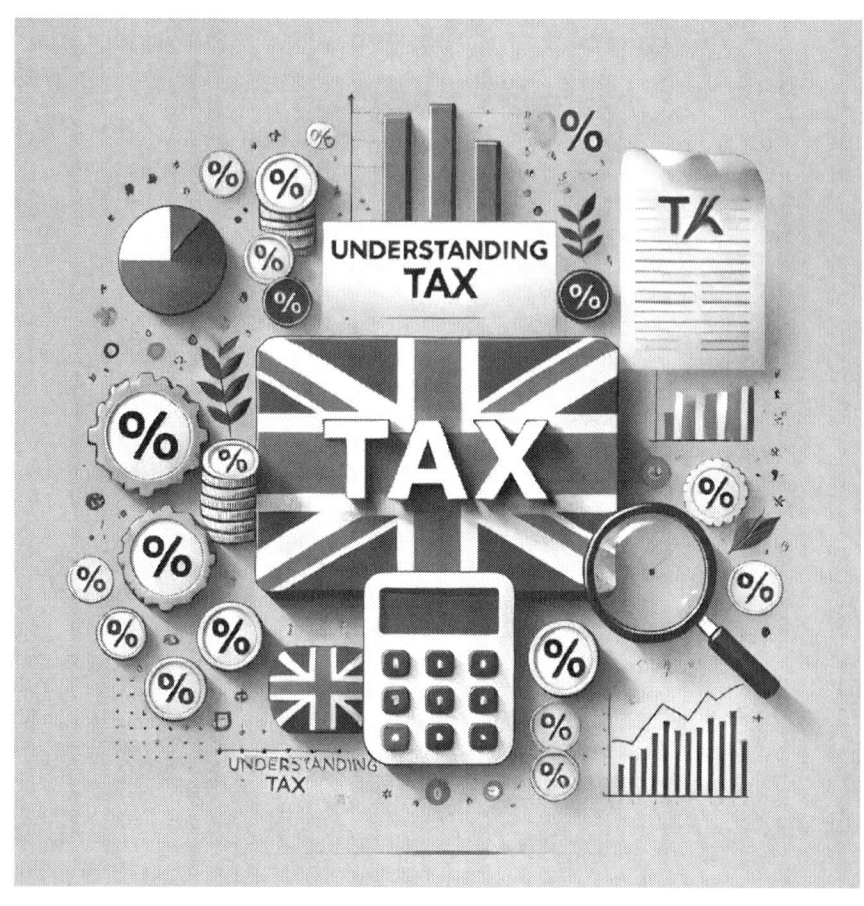

Chapter 3

Understanding UK Tax and National Insurance (NI)

Introduction: When you start earning money, you might feel a sense of excitement as you watch your pay arrive in your bank account. However, you'll quickly notice that the amount you receive is less than what you actually earned. That's because a portion of your income goes toward taxes and National Insurance (NI) contributions, which help fund essential services and benefits. While it might be frustrating to see part of your earnings go to the government, understanding how taxes and NI work will help you better manage your money and avoid any surprises in your pay cheque.

What is Tax? Tax is money that individuals, businesses, and even consumers must pay to the government. The government uses tax revenue to fund public services such as education, healthcare, transportation infrastructure, and emergency services. These services benefit everyone, and taxes make it possible for the government to provide them.

Taxes come in many forms, and some are applied to the income you earn, while others are applied to the goods and services you buy. Understanding the different types of taxes will help you grasp why taxes are important and how they affect your finances.

Income Tax: One of the most common taxes people pay is income tax. As the name suggests, income tax is a tax on the money you earn. If you have a job, are self-employed, or receive income from other sources, such as savings interest or rental properties, you are required to pay income tax.

The UK operates a progressive tax system, which means that the more you earn, the higher your tax rate will be. This ensures that people with higher incomes contribute more to public services. The tax system is divided into income tax bands:

- **Personal Allowance**: For the 2024/25 tax year, you can earn up to £12,570 without paying any income tax. This is known as your personal allowance.

- **Basic Rate**: Earnings above your personal allowance up to £50,270 are taxed at 20%.

- **Higher Rate**: Earnings between £50,271 and £125,140 are taxed at 40%.

- **Additional Rate**: For earnings above £125,140, the tax rate is 45%.

Income tax is deducted directly from your salary if you're employed, or you may need to file a tax return if you're self-employed or have other sources of income.

VAT (Value Added Tax): While income tax is deducted from your earnings, Value Added Tax (VAT) is applied to the goods and services you buy. VAT is a consumption tax that adds a percentage to the price of most products and services. For example, when you buy a new phone, part of the price you pay includes VAT.

In the UK, the standard VAT rate is currently 20%, but some goods and services, such as children's clothing and food, may have a lower VAT rate or be exempt from VAT altogether. VAT is an indirect tax, meaning you pay it as a consumer, and the businesses you buy from pass it on to the government.

What is National Insurance (NI)? National Insurance (NI) is another type of contribution that is deducted from your income, and it helps pay for key benefits that provide financial security throughout life. NI funds things like the state pension, unemployment benefits, and the National Health Service (NHS). While income tax is used to fund a wide range of public services, NI is specifically designed to support social security and healthcare systems.

NI contributions are deducted directly from your salary if you are employed, and if you are self-employed, you will need to calculate and pay your NI contributions through your tax return.

NI Contributions: There are several different classes of NI contributions, depending on your employment status:

- **Class 1**: Paid by employees and employers based on the employee's earnings. Employees pay NI once they earn above £242 per week, and employers also contribute.

- **Class 2 and Class 4**: Paid by self-employed individuals. Class 2 is a flat weekly rate for earnings above a certain threshold, while Class 4 is a percentage of profits above a higher threshold.

Like income tax, the more you earn, the more NI you contribute. The percentage of your income that goes to NI may vary depending on how much you earn and whether you are employed or self-employed.

How Much Tax and NI Will I Pay? As mentioned earlier, everyone in the UK has a personal allowance, which is the amount of income you can earn each year without paying tax. For the 2024/25 tax year, this amount is £12,570. If your income exceeds this amount, you will begin paying income tax on the portion that exceeds your personal allowance.

For National Insurance, contributions start once you earn more than £242 a week (as of the 2024/25 tax year). If you're self-employed, you'll need to manage your own NI payments, but for employees, your employer will automatically deduct NI from your pay cheque.

Why Taxes and NI Matter: At first glance, it might seem frustrating to see a portion of your hard-earned money being taken away for taxes and NI. However, taxes and NI play an essential role in keeping society running smoothly. They help fund critical services that everyone relies on, such as healthcare, schools, roads, and emergency services.

Understanding how taxes and NI work will help you budget your money better and plan for the future. When you know how much of your income will go towards taxes and NI, you can make more informed decisions about how much to save, spend, or invest.

Multiple Choice Questions:

1. **What is the primary purpose of income tax?**

   A) To fund public services

   B) To provide extra income to employers

   C) To reduce your salary

   D) To save for your retirement

2. **Which of the following is a progressive tax system?**

   A) A system where everyone pays the same tax rate

   B) A system where the tax rate increases as your income increases

   C) A system where taxes are not applied to income

   D) A system where only businesses pay taxes

3. **What is the VAT rate applied to most goods and services in the UK?**

   A) 15%

   B) 10%

   C) 20%

   D) 25%

4. What does National Insurance help fund?

A) Holidays for public employees

B) The state pension and the NHS

C) Government office supplies

D) Housing for civil servants

5. When do you start paying National Insurance in the UK?

A) When you earn more than £500 a week

B) When you are 18 years old

C) When you start a job

D) When you earn more than £242 a week

6. Why is it important to understand taxes and National Insurance?

A) To help you plan your finances and avoid surprises

B) To know how to avoid paying them

C) So you can get more money from your employer

D) So you can stop paying for public services

Chapter 4

What is Debt?

Introduction: Debt is a concept that most people will encounter at some point in their lives. It is essentially borrowing money that you will need to pay back later. Many people use debt to make significant purchases they can't afford to pay for upfront, such as a car or a house. However, while debt can help you achieve important financial goals, it can also lead to trouble if not managed carefully. Understanding what debt is, how it works, and how to manage it is crucial to avoiding financial pitfalls.

What is Debt? Debt occurs when you borrow money from a lender, typically a bank, financial institution, or credit provider, under the agreement that you will repay the borrowed amount - called the principal - along with interest. Interest is the fee you pay to the lender for borrowing the money, calculated as a percentage of the principal. The interest rate can vary depending on the type of debt, the lender, and your financial situation.

The most important thing to remember about debt is that it is not free money. You are obligated to repay both the principal and any accumulated interest. If not managed properly, debt can quickly grow and become overwhelming. That's why it's important to understand the different types of debt and how they work.

Types of Debt:

1. **Credit Card Debt**: When you use a credit card, you are borrowing money from the credit card company to make a purchase. If you pay back the full amount before your bill is due, you won't pay any interest. However, if you carry a balance from month to month, you will be charged interest on the remaining amount. Credit card interest rates can be high, often 20% or more, which means even small debts can grow quickly if you don't pay them off in full. It's easy to overspend when using credit cards, as the money isn't coming directly from your bank account at the time of purchase. This makes it crucial to track your spending and ensure you can pay off your balance each month.

2. **Personal Loans**: A personal loan is when you borrow a lump sum of money from a bank or lender, which you agree to pay back over a set period, typically in monthly instalments. Personal loans can be used for a variety of purposes, including home improvements, medical expenses, or consolidating other debts. The loan's interest rate may be fixed or variable, depending on the terms. Personal loans can be helpful for managing large expenses, but like credit card debt, they come with interest charges. The key is to ensure that you have a clear plan for repaying the loan on time.

3. **Overdrafts**: An overdraft occurs when you spend more money than you have in your bank account, and the bank covers the difference. Essentially, it's like borrowing a small loan from the bank for the amount you've overdrawn. Many banks allow customers to have arranged overdrafts, meaning you've pre-approved a limit with the bank, but even these come with interest charges and fees. Unarranged overdrafts, where you spend beyond your balance without pre-arranging the limit with the bank, often come with much higher fees and interest rates. Overdrafts are useful for short-term cashflow issues but should be avoided as a regular source of credit due to the high costs.

4. **Mortgages**: A mortgage is a specific type of loan used to buy property, usually a house. Mortgages are long-term loans, often lasting 25 to 30 years, and they usually involve borrowing large amounts of money. Because property is such an expensive purchase, mortgages allow people to spread the cost over many years. However, as with all loans, mortgages come with interest charges. Mortgages typically have lower interest rates than personal loans or credit card debt because they are secured loans. This means that the property itself is used as collateral - if you can't repay the mortgage, the lender can repossess your home to recover the debt.

5. **Student Loans**: In the UK, student loans are used to pay for university tuition fees and living expenses. These loans differ from other types of debt in that you only start repaying them once you earn above a certain income threshold after you graduate. The repayment terms are generally more flexible, and the interest rates are usually lower than those on credit cards or personal loans. Student loans are also unique because if your income never exceeds the threshold, or if you haven't paid off the loan after a set period (currently 30 years), the remaining balance may be forgiven.

The Risks of Debt: While debt can be a useful tool for managing big purchases or emergencies, it also comes with risks. If you borrow more money than you can afford to repay, debt can spiral out of control. High-interest rates, late fees, and penalties can quickly add up, making it difficult to escape the cycle of debt.

People who struggle to keep up with their debt payments may find their credit score damaged, making it harder to borrow money in the future. In extreme cases, excessive debt can lead to personal bankruptcy, which has long-lasting financial consequences.

How to Manage Debt: Managing debt responsibly is crucial to avoiding financial difficulties. Here are some key strategies to help you stay on top of your debt:

1. **Only Borrow What You Need**: Before taking on debt, carefully consider whether you truly need to borrow the money. Can you save up for the item instead? Borrowing only what you need ensures that you don't take on unnecessary debt.

2. **Understand the Terms**: Make sure you fully understand the terms of the loan, credit card, or overdraft before agreeing to it. Know the interest rate, any associated fees, and the repayment schedule. This knowledge will help you avoid surprises later on.

3. **Pay on Time**: Missing payments can lead to late fees and increased interest charges. Always make your payments on time, and if possible, pay more than the minimum amount to reduce your debt faster.

4. **Seek Help if Needed**: If you find yourself struggling with debt, don't hesitate to seek help. Many organisations offer free debt advice and counselling services. These professionals can help you create a plan to manage your debt and get back on track.

Multiple Choice Questions:

1. **What is the principal in a loan?**

    A) The total amount of interest you will pay

    B) The original amount of money borrowed

    C) The monthly payment you make

    D) The fee for borrowing money

2. **What happens if you don't pay off your credit card bill in full?**

    A) The debt is forgiven

    B) You are charged interest on the remaining balance

    C) You are automatically given a loan

    D) Nothing happens

3. **Which of the following is typically used to buy a house?**

    A) Credit card

    B) Overdraft

    C) Mortgage

    D) Personal loan

4. **When do you start repaying a student loan in the UK?**

    A) Immediately after taking out the loan

    B) Once you graduate and earn above a certain income threshold

    C) Before you start university

    D) Only if you fail to graduate

5. **What is a secured loan?**

    A) A loan that is backed by collateral, such as a house

    B) A loan where you don't have to repay the interest

    C) A loan that has no interest rate

    D) A loan with a fixed repayment date

6. **What is an overdraft?**

    A) Borrowing money using a credit card

    B) A personal loan for small expenses

    C) A type of mortgage

    D) Spending more money than you have in your bank account, which the bank covers

HOW CREDIT CARDS WORK

Chapter 5

Understanding How Credit Cards Work

Introduction: Credit cards are one of the most popular ways to pay for things in today's world. They offer convenience and flexibility, allowing you to make purchases without using cash and giving you the option to pay for those purchases later. However, with great convenience comes great responsibility. If not used carefully, credit cards can lead to significant debt and financial problems. Understanding how credit cards work will help you use them responsibly, avoid unnecessary fees, and build good financial habits.

How Credit Cards Work: When you use a credit card, you are essentially borrowing money from the credit card company. The credit card company pays the seller on your behalf, and you are then responsible for paying the credit card company back. This is why credit cards are considered a type of debt - you are borrowing money that you must repay, and if you don't repay it by the due date, you will likely have to pay additional interest and fees.

Unlike a debit card, which takes money directly from your bank account, a credit card allows you to make purchases even if you don't have enough cash at the moment. This can be useful in emergencies or when making large purchases, but it also means you must be careful not to spend more than you can afford to repay.

Credit Limit: Every credit card has a credit limit, which is the maximum amount of money you can borrow using that card. For example, if your credit limit is £1,000, you can spend up to £1,000 before you need to start repaying. Your credit limit is determined by the credit card company and is usually based on your credit score, income, and other financial factors. If you try to spend more than your credit limit, your card may be declined, or you may face additional fees.

It's important to remember that just because you have a high credit limit doesn't mean you should spend up to it. The more of your credit limit you use, the higher your debt will be, and the harder it can be to pay it off.

Billing Cycle: Your credit card activity is tracked over a billing cycle, which is usually about one month. At the end of each cycle, you receive a statement showing how much you've spent and how much you need to pay back. The statement will also include a due date by which you need to make at least the minimum payment to avoid penalties. The billing cycle is important because it determines when your payment is due and how interest is calculated. If you pay off your balance in full before the due date, you won't be charged any interest. However, if you carry a balance over to the next billing cycle, you'll start accruing interest on that balance.

Minimum Payment: Every credit card statement shows a minimum payment, which is the smallest amount you must pay to avoid late fees and penalties. While making the minimum payment will keep you in good standing with the credit card company, it's important to know that it won't clear your balance. Paying only the minimum means you will still owe money on the card, and interest will be charged on the remaining balance.

For example, if you owe £500 and your minimum payment is £25, you'll need to pay at least £25 by the due date. But if you only pay the minimum, you'll still owe £475, and the credit card company will charge you interest on that amount. Over time, paying only the minimum can make your debt grow quickly because of the added interest.

Interest Rates: Interest is the fee you pay for borrowing money on a credit card, and credit card interest rates are often much higher than the rates for other types of loans. If you don't pay off your balance in full by the due date, you will be charged interest on the remaining balance. Credit card interest is usually calculated daily, which means the longer you carry a balance, the more interest you will pay.

For example, if your credit card has an interest rate of 20% per year and you have a balance of £1,000, you could end up paying £200 in interest over the course of a year if you don't pay it off. That's why it's always best to pay off your balance in full each month to avoid paying interest.

Benefits of Credit Cards:

1. **Convenience**: Credit cards are widely accepted almost everywhere, whether you're shopping online, travelling abroad, or paying for everyday items like groceries. They also provide added

security, as you're not carrying cash, and most credit cards offer protection against fraud.

2. **Rewards**: Many credit cards offer rewards for spending, such as cashback, travel points, or discounts on purchases. For example, some cards give you 1% to 5% cashback on your purchases, which means you can earn money back just for using your card. Other cards offer points that can be redeemed for airline tickets, hotel stays, or other rewards.

3. **Building Credit**: Using a credit card responsibly can help you build a good credit score. A credit score is a number that represents your ability to manage debt, and it's important for future financial decisions, such as applying for a mortgage or car loan. By making your credit card payments on time and keeping your balance low, you can improve your credit score.

The Risks of Credit Cards:

1. **Debt**: It's easy to fall into debt with a credit card, especially if you spend more than you can afford to pay back. The high-interest rates on credit cards mean that small purchases can turn into large debts if they aren't paid off quickly. Debt can also negatively impact your credit score, making it harder to borrow money in the future.

2. **Fees**: Credit card companies charge various fees for things like late payments, going over your credit limit, or taking out cash advances. These

fees can add up quickly, making your credit card debt even harder to manage.

3. **Impact on Credit Score**: If you miss a payment or carry a high balance on your credit card, it can hurt your credit score. A low credit score can make it difficult to get approved for loans, rent an apartment, or even get a job in some cases.

How to Use Credit Cards Responsibly:

1. **Pay Off Your Balance in Full**: To avoid interest charges, always try to pay off your entire balance by the due date. This will help you stay debt-free and avoid paying extra money in interest.

2. **Keep Track of Your Spending**: It's easy to lose track of how much you've spent with a credit card, so make sure to monitor your purchases. Set a budget and stick to it, even if your credit limit is higher than what you can afford to repay.

3. **Avoid Cash Advances**: Taking out cash using your credit card often comes with very high fees and interest rates. Unless it's an emergency, avoid using your credit card for cash withdrawals.

4. **Check Your Statements**: Review your credit card statements regularly to make sure there are no unauthorised charges. If you notice any suspicious activity, report it to your credit card company immediately.

Multiple Choice Questions:

1. **What is a credit limit?**

    A) The amount of interest charged on a credit card

    B) The maximum amount you can borrow on a credit card

    C) The monthly fee for using a credit card

    D) The minimum amount you must pay each month

2. **What happens if you only pay the minimum payment on your credit card?**

    A) Your balance is cleared

    B) You don't have to pay interest

    C) Your credit limit increases

    D) You will be charged interest on the remaining balance

3. **What is one benefit of using a credit card?**

    A) You never have to repay what you spend

    B) It can help you build a good credit score

    C) You earn a salary for using it

    D) You avoid paying taxes

4. **How can you avoid paying interest on a credit card?**

   A) Pay off your balance in full every month

   B) Make only the minimum payment

   C) Spend below your credit limit

   D) Use your card only for large purchases

5. **What is a common risk of using a credit card?**

   A) Earning extra income

   B) Building credit

   C) Overspending and accumulating debt

   D) Avoiding interest

6. **What should you do if you notice unauthorised charges on your credit card statement?**

   A) Ignore them

   B) Report them to your credit card company immediately

   C) Pay them off to avoid interest

   D) Increase your credit limit

Chapter 6

Understanding Overdrafts

Introduction: An overdraft is a type of credit that allows you to spend more money than you currently have in your bank account. While it can be a helpful tool for managing short-term cashflow issues or handling unexpected expenses, it's important to understand how overdrafts work to avoid unnecessary costs and potential debt. Using an overdraft without fully understanding the fees, interest rates, and risks involved can quickly lead to financial problems.

What is an Overdraft? An overdraft occurs when you withdraw more money from your bank account than you have available. Instead of your payment being declined, your bank allows the transaction to go through, effectively lending you the money. This results in a negative balance, meaning you owe the bank money. Banks generally offer a specific overdraft limit, which is the maximum amount you can spend beyond your actual account balance.

For example, if your account balance is £0 and your overdraft limit is £500, you can still spend up to £500, even though you have no money in your account. While this can be convenient in emergencies, it's important to remember that overdrafts are a form of debt, and you'll need to repay the money you've borrowed, often with added interest and fees.

Types of Overdrafts:

1. **Arranged Overdraft**: An arranged overdraft is one that you set up with your bank in advance. The bank agrees to let you borrow money up to a specified limit, and you'll be charged interest on the amount you overdraw. The terms, such as the interest rate and fees, are usually lower than other types of debt because the bank has pre-approved your borrowing limit. This can be a useful tool if you occasionally need extra money for short-term needs, as long as you manage it carefully. For example, if you have an arranged overdraft limit of £300, you can spend that much even if your account is empty. While this can help cover unexpected expenses, it's essential to repay the overdraft as soon as possible to minimise interest charges.

2. **Unarranged Overdraft**: An unarranged overdraft occurs when you spend more money than you have in your account without agreeing on an overdraft limit with your bank. This can happen if you don't have an arranged overdraft or if you exceed your agreed limit. Unarranged overdrafts typically come with higher fees and interest rates because the bank wasn't expecting you to borrow this money. Banks may allow the transaction to go through, but you'll be charged significantly more than with an arranged overdraft, making this a much riskier option. Unarranged overdrafts can

also harm your relationship with your bank and affect your credit score if not managed properly.

The Costs of Using an Overdraft:

Using an overdraft isn't free. Banks charge interest on the amount you overdraw, and additional fees may apply, especially for unarranged overdrafts. The costs can quickly add up if you're not careful, so it's important to understand how these charges work.

1. **Interest Charges**: Most banks charge interest on the amount you overdraw, and this interest is typically calculated daily. The longer you remain overdrawn, the more interest you will pay. While interest rates on arranged overdrafts are often lower than those on credit cards, they can still be significant if you don't repay the overdraft quickly.

2. **Fees**: In addition to interest, banks may charge fees for using an overdraft. These fees vary depending on the bank and whether you're using an arranged or unarranged overdraft. For example, if you go into an unarranged overdraft, you may face daily fees or penalty charges. These fees can quickly increase the overall cost of borrowing, so it's important to be aware of your bank's policies.

When to Use an Overdraft:

Overdrafts can be helpful in certain situations, such as when you have unexpected expenses or need a temporary boost in cashflow. For example, if your rent payment is due but your pay cheque won't arrive until next week, an overdraft could cover the gap. However, overdrafts should be used sparingly and for short-term needs only. Relying on an overdraft as a regular source of credit can lead to costly fees and growing debt.

If you find yourself frequently needing to use an overdraft, it may be a sign that you need to revisit your budget and find ways to manage your money more effectively. Overdrafts are best used for emergencies, not everyday spending.

How to Manage an Overdraft:

1. **Only Use When Necessary**: Try to avoid using your overdraft unless absolutely necessary. Overdrafts should be reserved for emergencies or short-term needs, not for everyday expenses. Regularly relying on your overdraft can lead to financial difficulties and make it harder to break the cycle of debt.

2. **Repay as Soon as Possible**: If you use your overdraft, aim to repay the amount as soon as you can to minimise interest charges. The longer you stay overdrawn, the more expensive it becomes. Making regular payments to clear the balance will reduce your debt and lower the interest you owe.

3. **Check Your Bank's Terms**: Different banks have different rules for overdrafts, including interest rates, fees, and repayment terms. Make sure you understand your bank's terms before using an overdraft. This will help you avoid surprises and

ensure that you're aware of how much you'll need to pay.

4. **Set Up Alerts**: Many banks offer alert services that notify you when your account balance is low or when you're approaching your overdraft limit. These alerts can help you avoid accidentally going into an overdraft and incurring additional fees. Setting up notifications is a great way to stay on top of your finances and avoid unwanted charges.

The Risks of Overdrafts:

While overdrafts can be useful in emergencies, they come with significant risks. If you rely on your overdraft regularly, it's easy to fall into a cycle of debt. Each time you go overdrawn, you'll incur fees and interest, and the longer you remain in your overdraft, the more expensive it becomes.

1. **Cycle of Debt**: Once you start using an overdraft, it can be difficult to get back into the black. If you consistently spend more than you have, you may find yourself relying on your overdraft every month, accumulating more fees and interest charges along the way. Over time, this can lead to serious financial problems and make it harder to manage your money effectively.

2. **Impact on Credit Score**: Using an unarranged overdraft or failing to repay your overdraft can negatively affect your credit score. A lower credit score can make it harder to borrow money in the

future, whether you're applying for a loan, mortgage, or credit card. Banks and lenders look at your credit score to assess how reliable you are at managing debt, so it's important to use overdrafts responsibly to avoid damaging your credit.

Multiple Choice Questions:

1. **What is an overdraft?**

   A) A savings account

   B) A fee for using a debit card

   C) A type of credit that lets you spend more money than you have in your account

   D) A loan that doesn't need to be repaid

2. **What is the difference between an arranged and unarranged overdraft?**

   A) Arranged overdrafts are free, unarranged overdrafts charge a fee

   B) Arranged overdrafts are pre-agreed with the bank, unarranged overdrafts are not

   C) Unarranged overdrafts have lower interest rates

   D) There is no difference

3. **How can you avoid using an overdraft?**

   A) Always keep a close eye on your account balance

   B) Spend as much as possible

   C) Ignore bank alerts

   D) Rely on unarranged overdrafts regularly

4. What should you do if you use your overdraft?

A) Wait as long as possible to repay it

B) Repay the amount as soon as possible to minimise interest

C) Take out another overdraft

D) Avoid checking your account balance

5. What is one risk of relying on an overdraft?

A) You can avoid paying fees

B) Overdrafts are always free

C) Your credit score will automatically improve

D) You might fall into a cycle of debt

6. What can happen if you use an unarranged overdraft?

A) You'll be charged lower fees

B) Your credit score may improve

C) You could face higher fees and interest rates

D) The bank will pay you interest

Chapter 7

Personal Loans

Introduction: A personal loan is money you borrow from a bank, financial services company, or online lender that you agree to pay back over time, usually in monthly instalments. Personal loans can be used for various purposes, such as making a large purchase, consolidating existing debts, or covering unexpected expenses like property repairs. Understanding how personal loans work is crucial for making smart financial decisions and managing debt effectively.

How Personal Loans Work: When you take out a personal loan, you borrow a specific amount of money - known as the loan principal - and agree to repay it with interest over a set period. The loan term typically ranges from one to seven years. The interest rate you pay can be either fixed or variable:

- **Fixed Rate**: Your interest rate and monthly payments remain the same throughout the life of the loan, making it easier to budget and plan your finances.

- **Variable Rate**: Your interest rate and monthly payments may fluctuate over time, depending on market conditions. While you might benefit from lower payments if interest rates drop, you could also end up paying more if rates increase.

Terms of a Personal Loan: Understanding the key terms of a personal loan is essential before borrowing money:

- **Loan Amount**: The total amount of money you borrow.

- **Repayment Period**: The length of time over which you will repay the loan, typically between one and seven years.

- **Interest Rate**: The percentage of the loan amount that you pay in addition to the principal. A lower interest rate can save you money in the long term.

- **Fees**: Some personal loans come with fees, such as an arrangement fee, which is a one-time charge for processing the loan.

Types of Personal Loans: There are two main types of personal loans:

1. **Secured Loans**: These loans are backed by collateral, such as a car or savings account. If you fail to repay the loan, the lender can take the collateral as repayment. Secured loans typically have lower interest rates because they are less risky for the lender.

2. **Unsecured Loans**: These loans don't require collateral and are based on your credit history and income. Because they are riskier for lenders, unsecured loans often have higher interest rates.

When to Use a Personal Loan: Personal loans can be useful for various situations, including:

- **Debt Consolidation**: Combining multiple high-interest debts into one loan with a lower interest rate, making it easier to manage and pay off.

- **Major Purchases**: Financing large purchases like furniture, appliances, or electronics.

- **Home Improvements**: Paying for home renovations or repairs.

- **Unexpected Expenses**: Covering emergency expenses, such as car repairs.

The Risks of Personal Loans: While personal loans can be helpful, they come with risks:

- **Debt**: Taking out a loan means committing to regular monthly payments. If your financial situation changes, such as losing your job, you may struggle to make these payments.

- **Interest Costs**: The longer the repayment period, the more interest you'll pay over time, which can significantly increase the total cost of the loan.

- **Impact on Credit Score**: Missing loan payments or defaulting on the loan can damage your credit score, making it more difficult to borrow money in the future.

How to Choose a Personal Loan: When choosing a personal loan, consider the following:

- **Compare Offers**: Shop around and compare interest rates, fees, and loan terms from different lenders.

- **Read the Fine Print**: Make sure you understand all the fees and conditions before signing the loan agreement.

- **Borrow Only What You Need**: Avoid taking out a larger loan than necessary, as this will increase your debt and the amount of interest you pay.

Multiple Choice Questions:

1. **What is a personal loan?**

    A) A gift from the bank

    B) An account that earns interest

    C) A savings plan

    D) Money you borrow and agree to repay with interest over time

2. **What is the difference between a secured and unsecured loan?**

    A) Secured loans require collateral, unsecured loans do not

    B) Unsecured loans have lower interest rates

    C) Secured loans are given without credit checks

    D) There is no difference

3. **When might it be a good idea to take out a personal loan?**

    A) To buy daily groceries

    B) To consolidate high-interest debt

    C) To pay for small, everyday expenses

    D) When you don't need the money

4. **What is a key risk of taking out a personal loan?**

   A) Earning interest on your savings

   B) Increasing your debt and possibly paying high interest costs

   C) Getting a higher credit score automatically

   D) Never having to repay the loan

5. **What type of loan requires collateral?**

   A) Unsecured loan

   B) Fixed-rate loan

   C) Secured loan

   D) Variable-rate loan

6. **What should you do before signing a personal loan agreement?**

   A) Read the fine print and understand the fees and conditions

   B) Sign it quickly to get the money faster

   C) Take out more money than you need

   D) Ignore the interest rate

Chapter 8

The Different Types of Car Loans

Introduction: Buying a car is a major financial decision, and many people don't have enough savings to pay for it upfront. That's where car loans come in. A car loan allows you to borrow money to purchase a car and repay it over time. There are different types of car loans, each with its own advantages and disadvantages. Understanding these options can help you choose the best car loan for your needs and financial situation.

Types of Car Loans:

1. **Hire Purchase (HP)**: With a hire purchase agreement, you usually pay a deposit upfront (often around 10% of the car's price) and then make monthly payments over a set period, typically one to five years. During the repayment period, you are essentially "hiring" the car, and you don't own it until the final payment is made.

   o **Pros**: Lower monthly payments compared to some other options, and the interest rate is often fixed.

   o **Cons**: You don't own the car until the last payment is made, which limits your flexibility during the repayment period.

2. **Personal Contract Purchase (PCP)**: PCP is similar to hire purchase, but the monthly payments are typically lower, and there is a large final payment (often called a balloon payment) if you want to own the car at the end of the contract. Alternatively, you can return the car or trade it in for a new one.

   - ○ **Pros**: Lower monthly payments and flexibility at the end of the contract.

   - ○ **Cons**: The final payment can be very high if you want to own the car, and there are often mileage restrictions.

3. **Personal Loan**: You can also use a personal loan to buy a car. With a personal loan, you borrow the money from a bank or lender, purchase the car outright, and then repay the loan in monthly instalments. Since you buy the car outright, you own it from the start.

   - ○ **Pros**: You own the car immediately, and there are no mileage restrictions or conditions on how you use it.

   - ○ **Cons**: Monthly payments might be higher than with hire purchase or PCP, depending on the loan terms.

4. **Leasing**: Leasing a car is like renting it for a long period. You make monthly payments to use the car for a set time, usually two to four years. At the end of the lease, you return the car. Leasing often

includes servicing and maintenance, which can reduce additional costs.

- o **Pros**: Lower monthly payments and no concerns about the car's value at the end of the lease.

- o **Cons**: You never own the car, and there may be mileage limits and penalties for excessive wear and tear. Leasing can be more expensive in the long run if you keep leasing new cars.

Choosing the Right Car Loan:

When deciding on the best car loan for your needs, consider the following factors:

- **Monthly Payments**: How much can you afford to pay each month? Lower payments might seem appealing, but they could mean higher overall costs if there's a large final payment or if you lease the car.

- **Ownership**: Do you want to own the car at the end of the loan term? If owning the car is important to you, a hire purchase or personal loan might be a better option. If you prefer to change cars frequently, leasing or PCP might be more suitable.

- **Interest Rates**: Compare the interest rates of different loan options. A lower interest rate can save you money over the life of the loan.

- **Deposit Requirements**: Some loans require a deposit upfront. Make sure you have enough saved for a deposit if you choose an option like hire purchase.

The Risks of Car Loans:

Taking out a car loan means committing to regular monthly payments for several years. If your financial situation changes unexpectedly, you might find it difficult to keep up with the payments, putting you at risk of losing the car. Additionally, cars depreciate quickly, meaning they lose value over time. This could result in a situation where you owe more on the loan than the car is worth, especially with options like Personal Contract Purchase (PCP) or leasing.

Multiple Choice Questions:

1. **What is a key feature of a Hire Purchase (HP) agreement?**

   A) You own the car immediately after signing the agreement

   B) You hire the car and own it after making the final payment

   C) There is no deposit required

   D) Monthly payments vary depending on car usage

2. **What happens at the end of a Personal Contract Purchase (PCP) agreement?**

   A) You automatically own the car

   B) You must return the car to the dealer

   C) You can either make a final payment to own the car, return it, or trade it in

   D) The car is sold to someone else

3. **Which car loan option allows you to own the car outright from the beginning?**

   A) Leasing

   B) Personal Contract Purchase (PCP)

   C) Hire Purchase (HP)

   D) Personal Loan

4. **What is a common restriction associated with car leasing?**

   A) You must pay a large deposit

   B) You are limited in how many miles you can drive each year

   C) You own the car at the end of the lease

   D) There are no restrictions on car usage

5. **What is a balloon payment in a PCP agreement?**

   A) A large final payment to own the car at the end of the contract

   B) An extra fee for exceeding mileage limits

   C) The deposit you pay at the start

   D) A type of interest charge

6. **Which option offers lower monthly payments but may be more expensive long-term if you keep leasing new cars?**

   A) Hire Purchase (HP)

   B) Leasing

   C) Personal Loan

   D) Personal Contract Purchase (PCP)

Chapter 9

Understanding Mortgages

Introduction: A mortgage is one of the most important financial commitments many people will make in their lives. It is a loan used to purchase property, most often a home. Since homes are expensive, very few people can afford to buy one outright, so they take out a mortgage and repay it over many years. Understanding how mortgages work is essential if you plan to buy a home in the future. This chapter will explain the basics of mortgages, including the different types, how they work, and the risks involved.

How Mortgages Work: When you take out a mortgage, you borrow money from a lender, usually a bank or building society, to purchase a property. The lender provides the funds to buy the home, and in return, you agree to repay the loan over a set period, typically 25 to 30 years. The property itself acts as collateral, which means the lender has the right to repossess the home if you fail to make your mortgage payments. This ensures that the lender can recover its money if you default on the loan.

Deposit:

When you buy a home using a mortgage, you'll usually need to pay a deposit upfront, which is a percentage of the property's price. The deposit acts as a down payment, and the larger your deposit, the less money you'll need to borrow, and the lower your monthly payments will be. A typical deposit in the UK is around 5% to 20% of the property's value. For example, if you're buying a £200,000 home, you might need a deposit of £10,000 to £40,000, depending on the lender's requirements.

Interest Rates:

The interest rate on your mortgage is the cost of borrowing the money, and it plays a significant role in determining how much your monthly payments will be. There are two main types of mortgage interest rates:

- **Fixed Rate**: The interest rate remains the same for a set period, typically two to five years. This provides stability, as your monthly payments won't change during this time, making it easier to budget.

- **Variable Rate**: The interest rate can change over time, usually in response to changes in the Bank of England's base rate. This means your monthly payments could go up or down, depending on how interest rates fluctuate.

Repayment Types:

Most mortgages are repayment mortgages, which means you pay off both the loan (principal) and the interest each month. Over time, you reduce the loan balance, and by the end of the mortgage term, you'll have fully paid off the debt and own your home outright.

There are also interest only mortgages, where you only pay the interest on the loan each month. While this keeps your payments lower, you won't be paying off the loan itself. At the end of the mortgage term, you'll still owe the full amount you borrowed and will need a plan to repay it, such as selling the property or using savings.

Types of Mortgages:

1. **Fixed Rate Mortgage**: A fixed rate mortgage keeps the interest rate the same for a set period, usually between two and five years. This means your monthly payments will remain constant during this time, providing predictability and stability. Fixed rate mortgages are ideal if you want to avoid the risk of rising interest rates, but they may come with slightly higher rates compared to variable options.

2. **Variable Rate Mortgage**: A variable rate mortgage has an interest rate that can change over time, often in response to movements in the Bank of England's base rate. Your monthly payments could increase or decrease depending on how interest rates move. While you might benefit from lower rates when interest rates drop, your payments could also rise if rates increase, making it harder to budget.

3. **Tracker Mortgage**: A tracker mortgage is a type of variable rate mortgage where the interest rate is set at a fixed percentage above the Bank of England's base rate. For example, if the base rate

is 1% and your mortgage rate is 2% above the base rate, you'll pay 3% in interest. If the base rate rises or falls, your mortgage payments will adjust accordingly.

4. **Interest Only Mortgage**: With an interest only mortgage, you only pay the interest on the loan each month, not the principal. This keeps your payments low, but you will still owe the full loan amount at the end of the mortgage term. These types of mortgages are riskier because you must have a plan to repay the principal when the term ends, such as selling the property or using other investments.

The Costs of a Mortgage:

In addition to your monthly mortgage payments, there are other costs associated with getting a mortgage:

1. **Arrangement Fees**: Many lenders charge a fee to set up the mortgage. This can range from a few hundred to over a thousand pounds, depending on the lender.

2. **Valuation Fees**: The lender will often require a valuation of the property to ensure it's worth the loan amount. This fee covers the cost of the valuation.

3. **Legal Fees**: Buying a home involves legal processes such as conveyancing, which includes transferring the ownership of the property. These legal services come with fees.

The Risks of a Mortgage:

1. **Repossession**: If you fail to keep up with your mortgage payments, the lender can repossess your home to recover the loan amount. This is the biggest risk of taking out a mortgage, as you could lose your home if you can't make the payments.

2. **Interest Rate Increases**: If you have a variable-rate mortgage, your monthly payments could increase if interest rates rise. This could make your mortgage unaffordable if your income doesn't increase accordingly.

3. **Negative Equity**: If property prices fall, you could end up in negative equity, which means you owe more on your mortgage than your home is worth, which can make it difficult to sell or remortgage your home. This may not be a concern if you are still able to make the repayments on the mortgage.

How to Choose the Right Mortgage:

1. **Compare Offers**: Different lenders offer different mortgage rates and terms. Shop around to find the best deal that suits your financial situation.

2. **Consider Your Budget**: Make sure you can afford the monthly payments, even if interest rates rise. It's important to have a buffer in your budget for potential rate increases.

3. **Seek Advice**: A mortgage adviser can help you navigate the different options and find the mortgage that best suits your needs.

Multiple Choice Questions:

1. **What is a mortgage?**

    A) A loan used to buy property

    B) A type of savings account

    C) A fee paid to the bank

    D) An insurance policy for your home

2. **What is a deposit in the context of a mortgage?**

    A) The interest you pay on the loan

    B) The upfront payment you make when buying a property

    C) A monthly fee for using a bank account

    D) The total amount of the mortgage loan

3. **Which type of mortgage has a fixed interest rate for a set period?**

    A) Variable Rate Mortgage

    B) Interest Only Mortgage

    C) Fixed Rate Mortgage

    D) Tracker Mortgage

4. **What is a potential risk of a variable rate mortgage?**

   A) The interest rate remains the same

   B) Your monthly payments could increase if interest rates rise

   C) You never pay off the loan

   D) The bank sets a high deposit

5. **What is negative equity?**

   A) When you own more than one property

   B) When interest rates are lower than expected

   C) When you have paid off your mortgage early

   D) When your mortgage balance is higher than the value of your home

6. **What is a key benefit of a fixed-rate mortgage?**

   A) Payments stay the same, providing stability and predictability

   B) Interest rates drop automatically

   C) You don't have to repay the loan

   D) The interest rate changes each year

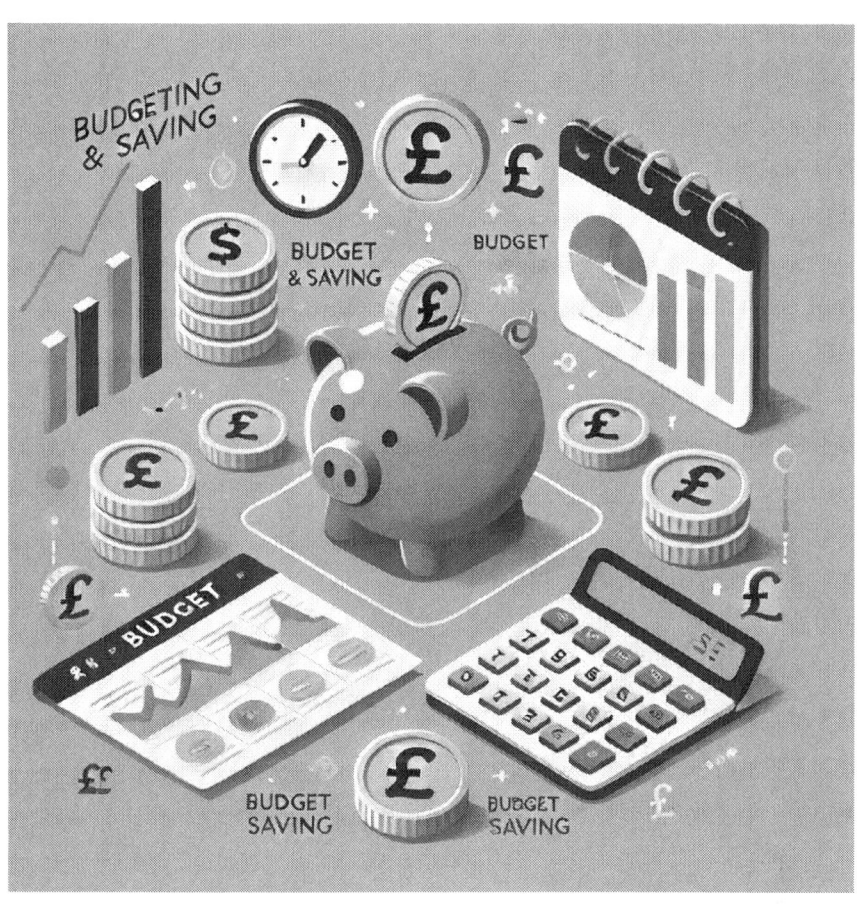

Chapter 10

Budgeting and Saving

Introduction: Budgeting and saving are essential life skills that help you manage your money wisely. Whether you're planning for a large purchase, trying to avoid debt, or simply looking to build financial security, understanding how to create and stick to a budget is key. Budgeting helps you make sure your money goes where it's needed, while saving ensures that you'll be financially prepared for the future. Together, these skills can help you take control of your finances, meet your financial goals, and avoid common financial pitfalls.

Why Budgeting is Important:

At its core, budgeting is about making a plan for how you'll spend your money. Without a plan, it's easy to lose track of where your money goes, and you might end up spending more than you earn. This can lead to financial stress, debt, and the inability to cover important expenses when they arise. Budgeting allows you to see your financial picture clearly. It helps you balance your income against your expenses, ensuring you have enough for both your essential needs (like food and rent) and your discretionary wants (like entertainment or new clothes). With a budget, you'll be able to save money more effectively, avoid unnecessary debt, and make informed financial decisions.

How to Create a Budget:

Creating a budget doesn't have to be complicated. By following a few simple steps, you can develop a budget that works for your lifestyle and financial situation.

1. **Track Your Income**: Start by identifying how much money you have coming in each month. This could be from a job, an allowance, or any other source. Knowing exactly how much money you make is the foundation of your budget.

2. **List Your Expenses**: Write down all your expenses, including necessities like rent, utilities, groceries, and transportation, as well as extras like eating out, subscriptions, and entertainment. Make sure to account for both fixed expenses (those that stay the same each month) and variable expenses (those that can change from month to month).

3. **Prioritise Your Spending**: Make sure your essential expenses are covered first. These are things you need to survive, such as food, housing, and transportation. After covering your essentials, set aside money for savings, and then allocate the rest toward discretionary spending (things you want but don't necessarily need).

4. **Set Savings Goals**: Decide how much you want to save each month. Your savings goals could be short-term, like saving for a holiday or new clothes, or long-term, like saving for a car, university, or even retirement. Building a habit of

saving regularly will help you meet both your short- and long-term goals.

5. **Stick to Your Plan**: A budget is only useful if you stick to it. Review your budget regularly to make sure you're on track, and make adjustments if needed. If you notice that you're consistently overspending in certain categories, find ways to cut back.

Saving Money:

Saving money is just as important as budgeting. By setting aside a portion of your income, you build financial security and make sure you're prepared for unexpected expenses. Different types of savings to consider are:

1. **Emergency Fund**: An emergency fund is money you save specifically for unexpected expenses, such as car repairs or sudden job loss. Financial experts recommend saving enough to cover three to six months of living expenses. Having an emergency fund ensures you won't have to rely on credit cards or loans in a financial emergency.

2. **Short-Term Savings**: These are savings for things you plan to buy in the near future, such as a new phone, a holiday, or a piece of furniture. Setting a short-term savings goal can help you avoid impulse purchases and give you time to plan your spending.

3. **Long-Term Savings**: Long-term savings are for bigger, more expensive goals, such as buying a

car, paying for university, or buying a house. These goals may take years to achieve, so it's important to start saving early and consistently.

Tools for Budgeting:

There are many tools available to help you manage your budget and track your spending. Here are a few popular options:

1. **Budgeting Apps**: There are various apps that can help you track your income, expenses, and savings in real-time. Popular options include Emma, Snoop, and Money Dashboard. These apps allow you to categorise your spending, set savings goals, and get notifications when you're close to exceeding your budget.

2. **Spreadsheets**: If you prefer a more hands-on approach, using a spreadsheet can be a simple and effective way to manage your budget. You can list your income, expenses, and savings goals, and adjust them as needed. Spreadsheets give you full control over your budgeting process.

3. **Envelopes**: The envelope method is a cash-based budgeting system. With this method, you divide your money into different envelopes, each labelled with a specific spending category (for example groceries, entertainment, transport). Once the money in an envelope is gone, you can't spend any more in that category until the next month.

Multiple Choice Questions:

1. **What is the first step in creating a budget?**

   A) Listing your expenses

   B) Tracking your income

   C) Setting savings goals

   D) Spending money

2. **Why is it important to have an emergency fund?**

   A) To cover unexpected expenses

   B) To buy a new phone

   C) To pay for a holiday

   D) To invest in stocks

3. **Which of the following is a tool you can use for budgeting?**

   A) Credit card

   B) Budgeting app

   C) Store loyalty card

   D) Gift card

4. **What should you do if your expenses are higher than your income?**

    A) Ignore the problem

    B) Borrow more money

    C) Adjust your budget by cutting non-essential expenses

    D) Increase your spending

5. **What is a short-term savings goal?**

    A) Saving for university tuition

    B) Saving for retirement

    C) Saving for a new phone or holiday

    D) Saving for a house deposit

6. **Which of these budgeting methods involves dividing money into specific categories for spending?**

    A) Using a credit card

    B) The envelope method

    C) Investing in stocks

    D) Tracking your income only

Chapter 11

Understanding Investments

Introduction: Investing is a powerful tool for growing your money over time. Unlike saving, which typically involves putting your money in a low-risk account with modest returns, investing allows you to put your money into financial products that have the potential to increase in value. While investing carries some risks, it also offers the opportunity for higher returns, helping you build wealth and reach your long-term financial goals.

What is an Investment?

An investment is something you buy with the expectation that it will increase in value over time, allowing you to make a profit when you sell it or earn money from it while you own it. Common types of investments include stocks, bonds, mutual funds, and real estate. The goal of investing is to make your money grow faster than it would in a standard savings account, which typically offers lower returns.

Types of Investments:

1. **Stocks**: When you buy a stock, you are purchasing a small piece of ownership in a company. As a shareholder, you benefit when the company does well - if the company's value increases, the value of your stock may rise, allowing you to sell it for a profit. However, stocks

also carry risk. If the company performs poorly or the market declines, the value of your stock could decrease, and you could lose money.

2. **Bonds**: A bond is essentially a loan you give to a company or government. In return, they agree to pay you interest over time and return the original amount you lent them (the principal) when the bond matures. Bonds are generally considered safer than stocks because they provide regular interest payments and have a fixed end date. However, they tend to offer lower returns compared to stocks.

3. **Mutual Funds**: A mutual fund pools money from many investors to buy a diversified portfolio of stocks, bonds, or other assets. This reduces the risk because your money is spread across a range of investments, rather than being tied to just one. Mutual funds are managed by professionals who make decisions about which assets to buy and sell, which can be helpful for new investors.

4. **Real Estate**: Investing in real estate involves buying property, such as houses or commercial buildings, with the hope that they will increase in value over time. You can earn money from real estate through rent or by selling the property for a profit. While real estate can offer high returns, it also requires a significant upfront investment and comes with ongoing costs, such as maintenance and property taxes.

Risk and Reward: All investments carry some level of risk, which is the possibility of losing money. Generally, the higher the potential return, the higher the risk. For example, stocks can offer high returns, but they can also lose value quickly if the market declines. On the other hand, bonds are more stable but typically offer lower returns. It's important to balance your desire for high returns with your ability to handle risk. This balance is called your risk tolerance.

Starting to Invest: You don't need a lot of money to start investing. Some platforms allow you to start with just a small amount of money and build your portfolio over time. Here are some key strategies for getting started:

1. **Start Small**: Begin with a small investment to get a feel for how the market works. As you become more comfortable, you can increase the amount you invest.

2. **Diversify**: Spread your money across different types of investments to reduce risk. This is called diversification, and it helps protect you if one investment performs poorly.

3. **Invest for the Long Term**: Investing is most effective when you leave your money to grow over a long period. Trying to "time the market" by buying and selling frequently can lead to losses, as it's difficult to predict short-term market movements.

Multiple Choice Questions:

1. What is a stock?

   A) A type of bond

   B) A loan to a company

   C) A small piece of ownership in a company

   D) A type of real estate investment

2. Which investment is generally considered safer but offers lower returns?

   A) Stocks

   B) Bonds

   C) Mutual funds

   D) Real estate

3. What does it mean to diversify your investments?

   A) To invest in different types of assets to reduce risk

   B) To put all your money in one stock

   C) To save all your money in a bank account

   D) To invest only in real estate

4. **What is a key strategy for successful investing?**

   A) Buying and selling frequently

   B) Investing for the long term

   C) Avoiding all risks

   D) Only investing in one company

5. **What is a mutual fund?**

   A) A loan to a company

   B) A type of bond

   C) A pool of money from many investors used to buy a diversified portfolio of assets

   D) A piece of real estate

6. **Which investment type involves buying property in hopes of increasing its value over time?**

   A) Stocks

   B) Bonds

   C) Mutual funds

   D) Real estate

Chapter 12

Understanding Insurance

Introduction: Insurance is a financial product that helps protect you from unexpected costs. Whether it's an accident, illness, or damage to your property, insurance can provide financial assistance when things go wrong. By paying a small amount of money regularly, called a premium, you transfer the risk of major financial losses to the insurance company. Understanding how insurance works and choosing the right type of insurance is an important part of financial planning.

What is Insurance? Insurance is essentially a contract between you and an insurance company. You agree to pay the company a regular premium, and in return, the company agrees to cover certain costs if something happens, like an accident, illness, or damage to your home. The idea behind insurance is to protect yourself from the financial impact of unforeseen events that could otherwise be very costly.

Types of Insurance:

1. **Health Insurance**: Health insurance helps cover the cost of medical expenses, such as doctor visits, hospital stays, and prescription medications. In the UK, the National Health Service (NHS) provides free healthcare to residents, but some people opt for private health

insurance to cover additional services or to receive faster treatment.

2. **Car Insurance**: Car insurance covers the cost of damage to your car and other vehicles involved in an accident. It also provides protection if your car is stolen or damaged in other ways. In the UK, car insurance is required by law, so if you drive, you must have at least third-party insurance, which covers damage to other people and their property.

3. **Home Insurance**: Home insurance protects your home and belongings from damage, theft, or natural disasters. There are two types of home insurance:

   o **Buildings Insurance**: Covers the structure of your home, including the roof, walls, and floors.

   o **Contents Insurance**: Covers your personal belongings, such as furniture, electronics, and clothing.

4. **Life Insurance**: Life insurance provides a financial payout to your family or other beneficiaries if you pass away. This money can be used to cover funeral costs, pay off debts, or help your family financially after you're gone.

How to Choose Insurance: When choosing an insurance policy, it's important to assess your needs and compare different options. Here are some tips to help you make the right choice:

1. **Understand Your Needs**: Think about what risks you need to protect against. For example, if you own a car, car insurance is essential. If you have a family, life insurance may be important to provide financial support in case something happens to you.

2. **Compare Policies**: Different insurance companies offer different coverage options and prices. Shopping around can help you find the best deal. Be sure to compare not only the cost but also the level of coverage and any exclusions.

3. **Read the Fine Print**: Make sure you understand what is and isn't covered by your insurance policy. Some policies may have exclusions or limits on what they will pay for, so it's important to read the details carefully.

The Role of Insurance in Financial Planning: Insurance is a key part of financial planning because it protects you from large, unexpected expenses that could otherwise lead to financial hardship. Without insurance, a serious illness, accident, or natural disaster could leave you with large bills that are difficult to pay. By having the right insurance, you can protect yourself and your family from these risks.

Multiple Choice Questions:

1. **What is the purpose of insurance?**

    A) To increase your savings

    B) To protect yourself from financial loss

    C) To earn interest on your money

    D) To avoid paying taxes

2. **Which type of insurance is required by law in the UK if you own a car?**

    A) Health Insurance

    B) Life Insurance

    C) Home Insurance

    D) Car Insurance

3. **What should you do before choosing an insurance policy?**

    A) Buy the first policy you find

    B) Skip reading the fine print

    C) Compare policies and understand your needs

    D) Only choose the cheapest option without considering coverage

4. **What does life insurance provide?**

   A) Money for a new car

   B) Coverage for home repairs

   C) Financial support to your beneficiaries if you pass away

   D) Money for a holiday

5. **What is a premium in an insurance policy?**

   A) The amount of money you receive from the insurance company

   B) The regular payment you make to keep the insurance active

   C) A penalty for making a claim

   D) A discount for buying multiple policies

6. **What is buildings insurance designed to protect?**

   A) The physical structure of your home, including walls and roof

   B) The contents of your home, such as furniture and electronics

   C) Your personal belongings outside the home

   D) Only the land your home is built on

Chapter 13

Managing Money in a Digital World

Introduction: In today's rapidly changing world, managing money has become increasingly digital. With the rise of online banking, mobile apps, and cashless payment methods, it's easier than ever to handle your finances without setting foot in a bank or using physical cash. However, the convenience of digital money management comes with its own set of challenges, such as cybersecurity risks. Understanding how to manage money in a digital world is essential for keeping your finances safe and efficient.

Digital Banking: Digital banking allows you to manage your money online or through mobile apps, giving you control over your finances from anywhere. With digital banking, you can:

- Check your account balance and transaction history

- Transfer money between accounts

- Pay bills and make purchases online

- Set up automatic payments or standing orders

- Deposit cheques using your phone's camera (in some cases)

Digital banking offers convenience and helps you stay on top of your money in real-time. It eliminates the need to visit a bank branch for routine transactions, and many banks now offer mobile apps with features that help you track your spending and manage your savings goals.

Cashless Payments: Cashless payments have become the norm in many places, allowing you to make purchases without using physical money. Here are some common cashless payment methods:

1. **Debit Cards**: Debit cards are linked directly to your bank account. When you make a purchase with a debit card, the money is taken from your account immediately. Debit cards help you avoid debt, as you can only spend the money you already have.

2. **Credit Cards**: Credit cards allow you to borrow money from the credit card company up to a certain limit. You can use the card to make purchases, and you'll be required to pay the money back later. If you don't pay off your balance in full each month, you'll be charged interest on the remaining amount.

3. **Digital Wallets**: Digital wallets, such as Apple Pay, Google Pay, and PayPal, store your payment information securely on your phone or online account. You can use these wallets to make payments quickly with your phone or online, without needing to enter your card details every time.

Cybersecurity: While digital banking and cashless payments offer convenience, they also expose you to certain risks, especially when it comes to protecting your financial information. Cybersecurity is essential for keeping your money and personal data safe. Here are some key practices to follow:

1. **Using Strong Passwords**: Create complex passwords that are difficult to guess. Use a mix of letters, numbers, and symbols, and avoid using the same password for multiple accounts.

2. **Enabling Two-Factor Authentication (2FA)**: Two-factor authentication adds an extra layer of security by requiring you to enter a second form of identification - like a code sent to your phone - along with your password.

3. **Being Cautious of Phishing Scams**: Phishing scams are fraudulent attempts to obtain your personal information, often through fake emails or messages. Be wary of any message that asks for your financial details, and avoid clicking on suspicious links.

The Rise of Cryptocurrencies: Cryptocurrencies, like Bitcoin and Ethereum, are digital forms of money that operate on blockchain technology. Unlike traditional currencies issued by governments, cryptocurrencies are decentralised and can be traded or used for certain online purchases. While they offer exciting possibilities, cryptocurrencies are highly volatile and risky. Their value can fluctuate dramatically in a short period, making them a less stable option for everyday use.

Multiple Choice Questions:

1. **What is digital banking?**

    A) Using online platforms and mobile apps to manage your money

    B) Managing your money with paper statements

    C) Using only cash for all transactions

    D) Avoiding all technology when managing money

2. **What is a digital wallet?**

    A) A physical wallet with cash

    B) An app that stores your card information for payments

    C) A savings account with a high interest rate

    D) A type of insurance policy

3. **What is a good cybersecurity practice?**

    A) Using the same password for all accounts

    B) Ignoring two-factor authentication

    C) Creating strong, unique passwords for each account

    D) Sharing your passwords with friends

4. **What is a cryptocurrency?**

   A) A type of credit card

   B) A digital form of money using blockchain technology

   C) A traditional bank loan

   D) A physical coin

5. **What is the main advantage of using digital banking?**

   A) You can only use it in one location

   B) It reduces your spending

   C) It helps you avoid online payments

   D) It offers convenience and real-time control of your finances

6. **Which payment method allows you to borrow money up to a limit, to be repaid later?**

   A) Debit card

   B) Digital wallet

   C) Credit card

   D) Cryptocurrency

Chapter 14

Planning for the Future

Introduction: Planning for the future is a critical part of managing your finances. Whether you're saving for university, a car, a home, or retirement, having a plan ensures that you're taking the necessary steps to achieve your financial goals. It also helps you prepare for the unexpected and build long-term financial security. By setting clear financial goals and understanding how tools like pensions work, you can make informed decisions that will benefit you in the years to come.

Setting Financial Goals: Financial goals give you something to work toward and help you stay motivated to save and invest wisely. These goals can be divided into three categories:

1. **Short-Term Goals**: These are goals you want to achieve within the next year or so, such as saving for a holiday, a new gadget, or a special event. Short-term goals are usually smaller amounts of money but still require planning and discipline.

2. **Medium-Term Goals**: Medium-term goals typically take between one and five years to achieve. These might include saving for a car, building up an emergency fund, or paying off a specific debt. Achieving medium-term goals often requires consistent saving and budgeting.

3. **Long-Term Goals**: Long-term goals are bigger, and they may take five years or more to achieve. These could include buying a home, paying for university, or building a retirement fund. Long-term goals require careful planning, patience, and long-term investment strategies.

Understanding Pensions: A pension is a special type of savings plan designed to help you save for retirement. In the UK, there are two main types of pensions:

1. **Workplace Pension**: A workplace pension is a retirement savings plan offered by your employer. Both you and your employer contribute a portion of your salary to your pension fund each month. The money is invested, and by the time you retire, you'll have a sum of money saved to help support you.

2. **State Pension**: The state pension is provided by the government and is paid to you once you reach the official retirement age, which is currently 66 in the UK. The amount you receive depends on how many years of National Insurance contributions you've made during your working life.

Saving for retirement might not seem urgent when you're young, but the earlier you start, the more time your money has to grow, making it easier to reach your long-term financial goals.

The Importance of Financial Education: Financial education is a lifelong process. The more you learn about money management, the better equipped you'll be to make informed decisions, avoid costly mistakes, and achieve financial independence. Topics like budgeting, saving, investing, and understanding taxes are all essential for building a secure financial future. Continuing to learn about these topics can help you make smarter financial choices and reach your goals faster.

Multiple Choice Questions:

1. **What is a financial goal?**

    A) A random expense

    B) Something you plan to achieve with your money in the future

    C) An unexpected bill

    D) A type of investment account

2. **What is a pension?**

    A) A savings plan for retirement

    B) A type of insurance

    C) A loan from the government

    D) A credit card

3. **Why is financial education important?**

    A) To avoid paying taxes

    B) To make informed decisions and achieve financial independence

    C) To learn how to spend more money

    D) To ignore budgeting

4. **What is an example of a long-term financial goal?**

   A) Saving for a holiday

   B) Eating out at a restaurant

   C) Purchasing a new phone

   D) Buying a house

5. **What does a workplace pension involve?**

   A) Only contributions from your employer

   B) A loan for retirement

   C) Contributions from both you and your employer

   D) A one-time payment

6. **What is a medium-term financial goal?**

   A) Saving for a car

   B) Buying a house

   C) Saving for a holiday next month

   D) Paying for retirement

Chapter 15

Financial Pitfalls to Avoid

Introduction: Managing your finances can be challenging, and many people fall into common traps that can lead to money problems. By understanding and avoiding these financial pitfalls, you can protect your financial wellbeing and work toward a more secure future. Whether it's overspending, ignoring debt, or falling victim to scams, learning how to navigate these risks will help you make smarter financial decisions.

Common Money Mistakes:

1. **Overspending**: Overspending happens when you buy more than you can afford, often by using credit cards or taking out loans. This can lead to debt, financial stress, and the inability to pay for essential needs. Many people overspend because they don't track their expenses or stick to a budget.

   Example: Emma loves shopping online, and she often buys clothes and gadgets without thinking about her budget. At the end of the month, she realises that she's spent more than she earns and can't afford to pay her credit card bill in full. As a result, she gets charged high interest and falls deeper into debt. If Emma had planned her spending and stuck to a budget, she could have avoided this situation.

2. **Ignoring Debt**: Debt can be overwhelming, but ignoring it only makes the problem worse. Failing to make payments on your debt can lead to late fees, higher interest rates, and damage to your credit score, which can affect your ability to borrow money in the future.

   Example: Matthew took out a personal loan to pay for his car, but he lost his job and couldn't keep up with the payments. Instead of reaching out to his lender to discuss a repayment plan, he ignored the problem. Over time, his debt grew due to interest and fees, and his credit score dropped. This made it harder for him to get another loan when he needed it. If Matthew had communicated with his lender and made partial payments, he could have avoided further financial trouble.

3. **Not Saving**: Many people underestimate the importance of saving money. Whether it's for emergencies or future goals, saving a portion of your income helps you prepare for unexpected expenses and gives you financial stability. Even small, regular savings can add up over time.

   Example: Emma spent most of her income on entertainment and dining out, leaving little for savings. When her car broke down, she didn't have enough money to cover the repair costs and had to borrow from a friend. If Emma had been saving a portion of her income each month, she would have had enough to cover the unexpected expense without borrowing.

4. **Impulse Buying**: Impulse buying is the act of making unplanned purchases, often driven by emotions or advertising. It can quickly drain your bank account and leave you with things you don't need. To avoid impulse buying, it's important to think carefully before making purchases and consider whether they fit into your budget.

   Example: Jake saw a new gaming console advertised online and decided to buy it immediately, even though he hadn't planned for it. Later, he realised he didn't have enough money to cover his rent for the month. If Jake had waited and evaluated whether he truly needed the console, he could have avoided this financial strain.

5. **Scams and Fraud**: Scammers use various tactics to trick people into giving up their personal or financial information. These scams can come in the form of fake emails, phone calls, or online offers that seem too good to be true. Falling for these scams can lead to identity theft, loss of money, and damage to your credit. It's important to be cautious and verify the legitimacy of any communication that asks for your financial information.

   Example: Lily received an email that appeared to be from her bank, asking her to verify her account information by clicking on a link. The email looked official, but it was actually a phishing scam designed to steal her personal data. If Lily had contacted her bank directly instead of clicking the link, she could have avoided the scam.

6. **The Danger of 'Buy Now, Pay Later'**: 'Buy Now, Pay Later' (BNPL) schemes allow you to purchase an item and pay for it in instalments over time. While this can be a convenient option, it's easy to accumulate debt if you're not careful. Many people use BNPL for purchases they can't afford, and if they fail to make the payments, they can face late fees and damage to their credit score.

   Example: Alex wanted a new TV but didn't have enough money to pay for it upfront. He used a BNPL service to spread the payments over several months. However, Alex didn't budget for the monthly payments, and soon he was missing payments and getting charged late fees. If Alex had waited until he could afford the TV or saved up for it, he wouldn't have fallen into debt.

Loan Sharks and Money Lenders: Understanding the Risks

What Are Loan Sharks?

Loan sharks are illegal money lenders who offer loans at extremely high interest rates and without proper authorisation. Unlike legal financial institutions, loan sharks operate outside of the law, and their lending practices can be predatory. They often target vulnerable individuals who may struggle to obtain credit from legitimate sources, taking advantage of their desperation for quick cash.

How Loan Sharks Operate

Loan sharks typically lend small amounts of money with no formal paperwork, but they demand repayment with exorbitant interest rates, making it nearly impossible for borrowers to pay off the debt. They may use intimidation, harassment, and even threats of violence to collect their money. These lenders do not follow any legal regulations or fair lending practices, making the loans not only risky but also dangerous.

The Consequences of Borrowing from a Loan Shark

The immediate access to money may seem tempting, but borrowing from a loan shark comes with severe long-term consequences:

- **Unmanageable Debt:** The high-interest rates charged by loan sharks can quickly spiral out of control, leaving borrowers trapped in a cycle of debt.

- **Harassment and Threats:** Loan sharks often use illegal methods to collect their payments, including harassment and violence.
- **No Legal Protection:** Since loan sharks operate illegally, borrowers have no legal protection if they fall victim to unfair practices.
- **Damage to Personal and Financial Wellbeing:** The stress and financial damage caused by loan sharks can impact a person's mental health, relationships, and long-term financial stability.

Legal Money Lenders: Know the Difference

Unlike loan sharks, legal money lenders are authorised by regulatory bodies, such as the Financial Conduct Authority (FCA) in the UK. These lenders are required to follow legal guidelines, including offering fair interest rates, transparent loan terms, and respecting borrowers' rights. Borrowing from a legal lender offers protection, and any disputes can be resolved through proper legal channels.

How to Protect Yourself

1. **Avoid Unregulated Lenders:** Always verify whether a lender is registered with an official regulatory authority before borrowing money.
2. **Know Your Rights:** Legal lenders must provide clear information about the interest rates, repayment terms, and any associated fees. If they don't, it's a red flag.
3. **Seek Legal Financial Advice:** If you are in a difficult financial situation, seek advice from

legitimate organisations like debt charities, financial advisers, or regulated lenders.

4. **Report Illegal Lending:** If you encounter or suspect a loan shark, report them to the relevant authorities. In the UK, the Illegal Money Lending Team is responsible for tackling loan sharks and protecting consumers.

Alternatives to Loan Sharks

If you're in need of money, consider safer alternatives:

- **Credit Unions:** These non-profit organisations offer low-interest loans to their members.
- **Payday Loans:** While also high-interest, payday loans are regulated and subject to legal oversight.
- **Debt Counselling:** Organisations like Citizens Advice or StepChange provide free debt advice and can help you find ways to manage your financial difficulties.

Multiple Choice Questions:

1. **What is a common financial mistake?**

   A) Living within your means

   B) Saving regularly

   C) Overspending

   D) Planning for the future

2. **Why should you avoid ignoring debt?**

   A) Because it will go away on its own

   B) Because it can lead to more interest charges and financial trouble

   C) Because it increases your income

   D) Because it's not important

3. **What should you do if you receive a suspicious email asking for your financial information?**

   A) Delete the email and do not respond

   B) Provide the information immediately

   C) Share the email with your friends

   D) Click on all links in the email

4. **What is a potential risk of using 'Buy Now, Pay Later' schemes?**

   A) Earning extra income

   B) Falling into debt if you can't afford the payments

   C) Saving money on purchases

   D) Automatically improving your credit score

5. **What is the best way to avoid impulse buying?**

   A) Buy things as soon as you see them

   B) Use a credit card for all purchases

   C) Think carefully about whether you need something before purchasing

   D) Avoid creating a budget

6. **What is a key reason for building an emergency fund?**

   A) To cover unexpected expenses like car repairs

   B) To buy luxury items

   C) To take out loans in the future

   D) To make large impulse purchases

Chapter 16

Understanding Your Credit Score

Introduction: Your credit score is one of the most important numbers in your financial life. It's a numerical representation of your creditworthiness, which essentially reflects how responsible and reliable you are when it comes to borrowing and repaying money. Lenders, banks, landlords, and even some employers use your credit score to decide whether to lend you money, approve you for a mortgage, or offer you a rental agreement. Understanding your credit score and knowing how to manage it effectively is essential for maintaining a strong financial profile throughout your life.

Whether you're applying for a new credit card, looking to rent a flat, or seeking approval for a car loan, your credit score plays a critical role. A good credit score can lead to lower interest rates, better loan terms, and more financial opportunities, while a poor score can limit your options and cost you more in the long run. In this chapter, we'll dive deeper into what a credit score is, why it's important, how to improve it, and the impact a poor score can have on your financial wellbeing.

What is a Credit Score?

A credit score is a three-digit number that represents a summary of your credit history and financial behaviour. In the UK, credit scores typically range from 300 to 999, depending on the credit reference agency. The higher the number, the better your credit score is considered, and the more likely you are to be seen as a reliable borrower. Conversely, a lower score may indicate that you've had trouble managing credit in the past or are currently facing financial difficulties.

Your credit score is calculated based on several key factors:

- **Payment History:** This is one of the most significant factors. Lenders want to see if you've paid past credit accounts on time. Late payments, missed payments, or defaults can severely hurt your score.

- **Credit Utilisation:** This refers to how much of your available credit you're using. A lower percentage of credit usage suggests that you're managing your credit well, whereas maxing out your credit cards can signal financial distress.

- **Length of Credit History:** The longer your credit history, the better. Lenders like to see that you have experience managing credit over time.

- **Types of Credit:** Having a mix of credit types (for example credit cards, personal loans, and mortgages) can help your score, as it shows lenders you can handle different types of credit responsibly.

- **Recent Credit Applications:** Applying for several credit accounts in a short period can negatively affect your score, as it suggests you may be desperate for credit or planning to take on more debt than you can handle.

Why Is Your Credit Score Important?

Your credit score impacts many aspects of your financial life. Here are some of the key ways in which it affects you:

1. **Getting Loans and Mortgages:** When you apply for a loan or a mortgage, lenders use your credit score to determine how likely you are to repay the money they lend you. A higher credit score can make you eligible for better loan terms, such as lower interest rates and higher loan amounts. A lower score, however, may result in higher interest rates or even outright denial of your application.

   Example: Emily is looking to buy her first home. With a credit score of 820, she's offered a mortgage with a low interest rate, which saves her thousands of pounds over the life of the loan. Her friend James, with a credit score of 620, is approved for a mortgage as well, but at a much higher interest rate, meaning he'll pay significantly more in interest over time.

2. **Renting Property:** Landlords often check potential tenants' credit scores to assess whether they are likely to pay rent on time. A high credit score can help you secure a rental property more easily, while a low score might make landlords hesitant to rent to you or ask for a larger deposit upfront.

3. **Getting a Mobile Phone Contract:** Mobile phone providers often run credit checks before approving you for a contract. If you have a low credit score, you may be denied a contract or required to pay a larger deposit or prepay for services.

4. **Job Applications:** In certain sectors, especially finance, employers may check your credit score as part of the hiring process. This is because they want to ensure that you are responsible and can manage your own finances before trusting you with the company's.

How to Improve Your Credit Score:

Improving your credit score takes time and effort, but it's worth it. A higher credit score not only makes it easier to get approved for loans and credit cards, but it also saves you money through lower interest rates. Here are some key strategies to improve your credit score:

1. **Pay Your Bills on Time:** Your payment history is one of the most significant factors that impact your credit score. Even one missed payment can have a negative effect, so it's crucial to stay on top of your bills, including credit cards, loans, utilities, and any other recurring payments. **Tip:** Set up automatic payments for bills to ensure you never miss a due date. Alternatively, use calendar reminders or alerts to help keep track of payment deadlines.

2. **Reduce Your Debt:** The amount of debt you owe plays a major role in your credit score. Credit utilisation refers to the amount of your available credit that you're using. Ideally, you should aim to keep your credit utilisation ratio below 30% - this means using no more than 30% of your total credit limit. High balances on credit cards can signal that you're over-reliant on credit, which can hurt your score.

    Tip: Pay high-interest debts first, as this will save you more in interest payments and improve your credit score faster. Avoid maxing out your credit cards and consider spreading out your spending over multiple cards to keep utilisation low.

3. **Don't Apply for Too Much Credit at Once:** Every time you apply for a new credit card or loan, the lender performs a hard inquiry on your credit report. Too many hard inquiries in a short period can lower your score, as it indicates to lenders that you may be taking on more debt than you can manage.
    Tip: Be strategic about applying for new credit. Only apply when you really need it and avoid opening multiple accounts in a short time frame.

4. **Build a Long Credit History:** The length of your credit history is another key factor in your credit score. The longer you've been managing credit responsibly, the better. If you're new to credit or haven't used it much, it may take some time to build up your credit score.

Tip: Even if you don't use a credit card regularly, keeping it open and occasionally making small purchases can help lengthen your credit history. Avoid closing old accounts, as this can reduce the length of your overall credit history.

5. **Check Your Credit Report Regularly:** It's important to keep an eye on your credit report to catch any errors or signs of fraud that could negatively impact your score. Mistakes, such as incorrect personal details or unauthorised transactions, can drag your score down if not addressed.

   Tip: You're entitled to check your credit report for free once a year from each of the main credit reference agencies (Experian, Equifax, and TransUnion). Regularly reviewing your report ensures you can dispute errors and correct any inaccuracies.

   The Impact of a Bad Credit Score:

   Having a low credit score can limit your financial opportunities and cost you more money in the long run. Here's how:

1. **Higher Interest Rates:** Lenders see borrowers with low credit scores as riskier, so they charge higher interest rates to offset the risk. This means you'll end up paying more in interest over the life of a loan or credit card balance, which can strain your finances.

2. **Difficulty Getting Approved for Loans:** With a low credit score, you may struggle to get approved for loans, credit cards, or mortgages. Even if you are approved, the loan terms may be less favourable, making it harder to borrow money when you need it most.

3. **Trouble Renting or Buying a Home:** A poor credit score can make it difficult to rent a flat or secure a mortgage. Landlords may be hesitant to rent to someone with a low score, and mortgage lenders might reject your application or offer you a loan with high interest rates.

4. **Limited Access to Credit Cards and Contracts:** Credit card companies and mobile phone providers may deny you access to their products if your credit score is too low. This can limit your ability to get essential services, such as a mobile phone contract or a credit card for emergencies.

Multiple Choice Questions:

1. **What is a credit score?**

    A) A number that shows how much money you have in the bank

    B) A three-digit number that shows your creditworthiness

    C) A record of your employment history

    D) The amount of money you owe to friends

2. **Why is it important to have a good credit score?**

    A) To avoid paying taxes

    B) To get lower interest rates and better financial opportunities

    C) To increase your monthly income

    D) To qualify for student loans

3. **What can help improve your credit score?**

    A) Paying your bills late

    B) Applying for multiple credit cards at once

    C) Paying off debt and keeping your credit utilisation low

    D) Closing old credit accounts

4. **What is the credit utilisation ratio?**

A) The amount of debt you carry compared to your credit limits

B) The number of credit cards you have

C) The percentage of your income that goes toward rent

D) The total amount of money you spend each month

4. **What is one reason to check your credit report regularly?**

A) To apply for more credit cards

B) To find mistakes or unauthorised transactions and dispute them

C) To avoid paying your bills

D) To improve your credit score automatically

5. **What is a potential impact of a bad credit score?**

A) Lower interest rates

B) Better job opportunities

C) Higher interest rates and difficulty getting loans

D) Access to more credit cards

132

Chapter 17

Financial Responsibilities as an Adult

Introduction: As you grow older, your financial responsibilities will change and evolve. While you may have started with saving money or using a debit card in your teens, adulthood brings a new set of financial obligations. These include paying bills, managing taxes, taking out loans, and making important decisions like renting or buying a home. In this chapter, we will explore the key financial responsibilities you'll encounter as an adult and how to navigate them successfully.

1. Earning and Managing Income:

Once you start earning a full-time salary, managing your income becomes essential. Whether you're paid weekly, bi-weekly, or monthly, you'll need to budget for your expenses and savings to ensure your money lasts until the next pay cheque.

Budgeting:
Creating a monthly budget is crucial as an adult. You'll need to plan for essential expenses like rent or mortgage payments, utilities, groceries, transport, and savings. It's also important to set aside money for discretionary spending, such as entertainment, dining out, and hobbies.

Taxes:
As an adult, you will be required to pay income taxes.

This will either be deducted automatically through your pay cheque if you're employed (via PAYE in the UK), or you'll need to submit a tax return if you're self-employed. Understanding tax bands and how to optimise your earnings for tax efficiency (like using tax-free savings accounts) becomes increasingly important.

2. Renting vs. Buying a Home:

One of the most significant financial decisions you'll make is where you live. Many adults start by renting a home or flat, while others may choose to buy property if they can afford the deposit and mortgage payments.

Renting a Home:
Renting can be more flexible, especially if you're not sure where you want to settle down or if you're still in the early stages of your career. When renting, you'll need to budget for a security deposit, rent payments, and possibly utilities. Your credit score may also be checked by landlords to ensure you're financially stable.

Buying a Home:
Buying property can be a great long-term investment, but it comes with responsibilities. You'll need a mortgage, which is a loan used to buy the property, and you'll make monthly payments over many years. Additionally, owning a home means paying for maintenance, property taxes, and homeowners' insurance.

Example:
Sophie is considering whether to rent or buy. Renting gives her more flexibility to move to a different city for job opportunities, but buying a home allows her to build

equity (the portion of the property she owns) over time. After budgeting and considering her long-term goals, Sophie decides to rent for now, with the plan to save for a home in the future.

3. Utilities and Monthly Bills:

As an adult, you'll be responsible for a range of monthly bills. These include:

- **Electricity and Gas:** These are basic utilities required to power and heat your home.

- **Water Bills:** Many areas require payment for water and sewage services.

- **Internet and Phone:** Access to the internet and mobile phones is essential, and these services come with monthly fees.

- **Council Tax (UK):** If you're living in a property, you'll be required to pay council tax, which funds local services like waste collection and public facilities.

You must ensure these bills are paid on time each month to avoid penalties and additional charges.

4. Health Insurance and Healthcare Costs:

In many countries, you'll need to plan for healthcare costs. In the UK, the NHS provides healthcare services, but some people choose private health insurance for additional coverage or faster access to treatments. In countries like the US, private health insurance is essential to cover medical bills. As an adult, it's important to budget for healthcare expenses, including health insurance premiums, prescriptions, and other medical costs.

5. Saving for Retirement:

Planning for retirement may seem far away, but the earlier you start, the more time your money has to grow. Many employers in the UK offer workplace pensions, where both you and your employer contribute. If you have access to a workplace pension including auto-enrolment then it should be taken up, as the employer will be contributing to your pension – in general, opting out is not a good strategy for long term security

It's worth being aware that a workplace pension may need supplementing if a good quality of life in retirement is being sought. You can also contribute to private pension plans or Individual Savings Accounts (ISAs) in the UK to grow your retirement savings.

Example:
James is in his late 20s and recently started a full-time job. His employer offers a workplace pension, and James decides to contribute a percentage of his salary each month. By doing this, he takes advantage of employer contributions, and over time, his pension pot grows, ensuring he'll have funds for retirement.

6. Borrowing and Credit:

As an adult, you may need to take out loans for significant expenses such as buying a car or home improvements. It's important to manage loans responsibly and to understand the terms and conditions before signing any agreements. Your credit score will also play a significant role in your ability to borrow money and the interest rates you receive.

- **Loans and Mortgages:** Borrowing money in the form of personal loans or mortgages can help you purchase large assets, but you'll need to repay the money with interest. Ensure that you understand the terms of the loan and how much interest you will be paying over time.

- **Credit Cards:** Using credit cards responsibly is another key financial responsibility. Always aim to pay off your balance in full each month to avoid paying interest.

Multiple Choice Questions:

1. **What is one of the key responsibilities of managing income as an adult?**

    A) Spending without tracking

    B) Creating a budget to cover expenses and savings

    C) Borrowing as much money as possible

    D) Avoiding paying taxes

2. **What is the main difference between renting and buying a home?**

    A) Renting requires a deposit, but buying does not

    B) Buying is more flexible than renting

    C) Renting allows flexibility, while buying builds long-term equity

    D) Both renting and buying come with no monthly payments

3. **Which of the following is a utility bill that must be paid regularly?**

    A) Gym membership

    B) Internet and phone services

    C) Credit card balance

    D) Travel expenses

4. **What is an advantage of contributing to a workplace pension?**

> A) Your employer also contributes, helping your pension grow
>
> B) You only contribute when you feel like it
>
> C) You can withdraw all the money anytime
>
> D) It only benefits those over 50

5. **Why is it important to understand loan terms before borrowing?**

> A) To borrow as much as possible
>
> B) So you can transfer the loan to someone else
>
> C) To avoid repaying the loan
>
> D) To ensure you know how much interest you will pay and how long it will take to repay the loan

6. **What is one consequence of not paying your utility bills on time?**

> A) Your credit score will improve
>
> B) You'll receive a discount
>
> C) You may face penalties, fees, and possibly lose service
>
> D) The bill will be automatically forgiven

Multiple Choice Answers

Chapter 1

Answers:

1. A) Trading goods and services

2. B) You can save money and use it later without losing its value

3. C) Barter system

4. C) A loan from a bank

5. B) To avoid carrying heavy metal coins

6. D) Cryptocurrency

Chapter 2

1. B) Salaries are fixed amounts, while wages are based on the hours worked

2. C) You run your own business and are responsible for managing your income

3. B) Earning money from investments or property rentals

4. C) They work on short-term projects for multiple clients

5. B) Skills increase your ability to earn more money and advance in your career

6. B) It allows people to earn money online and work remotely

Chapter 3

1. A) To fund public services

2. B) A system where the tax rate increases as your income increases

3. C) 20%

4. B) The state pension and the NHS

5. D) When you earn more than £242 a week

6. A) To help you plan your finances and avoid surprises

Chapter 4

1. B) The original amount of money borrowed

2. B) You are charged interest on the remaining balance

3. C) Mortgage

4. B) Once you graduate and earn above a certain income threshold

5. A) A loan that is backed by collateral, such as a house

6. D) Spending more money than you have in your bank account, which the bank covers

Chapter 5

1. B) The maximum amount you can borrow on a credit card

2. D) You will be charged interest on the remaining balance

3. B) It can help you build a good credit score

4. A) Pay off your balance in full every month

5. C) Overspending and accumulating debt

6. B) Report them to your credit card company immediately

Chapter 6

1. C) A type of credit that lets you spend more money than you have in your account

2. B) Arranged overdrafts are pre-agreed with the bank, unarranged overdrafts are not

3. A) Always keep a close eye on your account balance

4. B) Repay the amount as soon as possible to minimise interest

5. D) You might fall into a cycle of debt

6. C) You could face higher fees and interest rates

Chapter 7

1. D) Money you borrow and agree to repay with interest over time

2. A) Secured loans require collateral, unsecured loans do not

3. B) To consolidate high-interest debt

4. B) Increasing your debt and possibly paying high interest costs

5. C) Secured loan

6. A) Read the fine print and understand the fees and conditions

Chapter 8

1. B) You hire the car and own it after making the final payment

2. C) You can either make a final payment to own the car, return it, or trade it in

3. D) Personal Loan

4. B) You are limited in how many miles you can drive each year

5. A) A large final payment to own the car at the end of the contract

6. B) Leasing

Chapter 9

1. A) A loan used to buy property

2. B) The upfront payment you make when buying a property

3. C) Fixed-Rate Mortgage

4. B) Your monthly payments could increase if interest rates rise

5. D) When your mortgage balance is higher than the value of your home

6. A) Payments stay the same, providing stability and predictability

Chapter 10

1. B) Tracking your income

2. A) To cover unexpected expenses

3. B) Budgeting app

4. C) Adjust your budget by cutting non-essential expenses

5. C) Saving for a new phone or holiday

6. B) The envelope method

Chapter 11

1. C) A small piece of ownership in a company

2. B) Bonds

3. A) To invest in different types of assets to reduce risk

4. B) Investing for the long term

5. C) A pool of money from many investors used to buy a diversified portfolio of assets

6. D) Real estate

Chapter 12

1. B) To protect yourself from financial loss

2. D) Car Insurance

3. C) Compare policies and understand your needs

4. C) Financial support to your beneficiaries if you pass away

5. B) The regular payment you make to keep the insurance active

6. A) The physical structure of your home, including walls and roof

Chapter 13

1. A) Using online platforms and mobile apps to manage your money

2. B) An app that stores your card information for payments

3. C) Creating strong, unique passwords for each account

4. B) A digital form of money using blockchain technology

5. D) It offers convenience and real-time control of your finances

6. C) Credit card

Chapter 14

1. B) Something you plan to achieve with your money in the future

2. A) A savings plan for retirement

3. B) To make informed decisions and achieve financial independence

4. D) Buying a house

5. C) Contributions from both you and your employer

6. A) Saving for a car

Chapter 15

1. C) Overspending

2. B) Because it can lead to more interest charges and financial trouble

3. A) Delete the email and do not respond

4. B) Falling into debt if you can't afford the payments

5. C) Think carefully about whether you need something before purchasing

6. A) To cover unexpected expenses like car repairs

Chapter 16

1. B) A three-digit number that shows your creditworthiness

2. B) To get lower interest rates and better financial opportunities

3. C) Paying off debt and keeping your credit utilisation low

4. A) The amount of debt you carry compared to your credit limits

5. B) To find mistakes or unauthorised transactions and dispute them

6. C) Higher interest rates and difficulty getting loans

Chapter 17

1. B) Creating a budget to cover expenses and savings

2. C) Renting allows flexibility, while buying builds long-term equity

3. B) Internet and phone services

4. A) Your employer also contributes, helping your pension grow

5. D) To ensure you know how much interest you will pay and how long it will take to repay the loan

6. C) You may face penalties, fees, and possibly lose service

Conclusion

Congratulations on completing this journey into the world of money! By now, you've gained valuable insights into what money is, how it's earned, and the vital role it plays in our everyday lives. You've explored essential topics like budgeting, saving, investing, and managing debt, all of which are key to making informed and responsible financial decisions.

Understanding money is one of the most important skills you can develop. Whether you're preparing for your first job, saving for something special, or planning your long-term future, the knowledge you've gathered from this book will guide you in making smart choices. Money is a tool that, when managed wisely, can help you achieve your goals and live a life of financial independence.

But remember, this is just the beginning. The world of finance is ever-evolving, and there's always more to learn. Stay curious, continue asking questions, and keep educating yourself on new financial trends and strategies. The more you understand, the better equipped you'll be to face financial challenges and seize opportunities as they arise.

As you move forward, here are some key lessons to keep in mind:

- **Budget Wisely:** Always keep track of your spending. Ensure that you're living within your means and that you're not spending more than you earn.

- **Save Regularly:** Set aside money for the future, whether it's for a short-term goal or a long-term need. Building savings is the foundation of financial security.

- **Invest Carefully:** Learn about different ways to grow your money, but always be aware of the risks. Diversify your investments to protect against potential losses.

- **Use Credit Responsibly:** Understand the costs of borrowing and be sure you can repay what you owe. Credit can be helpful, but it can also lead to debt if mismanaged.

- **Plan Ahead:** Whether it's for further education, buying a home, or retirement, having a clear financial plan will help you stay focused on achieving your goals.

Finally, remember that financial success is not measured by how much money you have, but by how well you manage and use it to support your life goals. With the knowledge and skills you've acquired, you are now better prepared to make smart financial decisions that will guide you toward a secure and fulfilling future.

Thank you for taking the time to learn these essential financial principles. Your future self will undoubtedly be grateful for the steps you're taking now to build a strong financial foundation. Now, go forward and take control of your financial destiny!

Wishing you success and prosperity,
Karl Hartey

About The Author

Karl Hartey is a renowned author, professional speaker, philanthropist, and one of the UK's leading experts in financial planning. As an ISO22222 qualified financial planner, a distinction held by fewer than 100 advisers in the UK at the time of print, Karl brings a unique combination of expertise and passion to the world of finance.

His commitment to financial education has culminated in the creation of the highly regarded "All You Need to Know About Money" series, comprising seven insightful books that guide readers through the complexities of personal finance. Karl's ability to break down complicated financial principles into practical, understandable advice has made him a sought-after international speaker, empowering individuals across the globe to take control of their financial futures.

As a philanthropist, Karl serves as a trustee of the Charlotte Hartey Foundation, a charity dedicated to helping children and teenagers. Through his foundation work, he continues to give back to the community by supporting youth development, education, and wellbeing.

Karl's personal motivation is simple yet powerful: to change one life at a time through financial education. His work is driven by a deep belief in the transformative power of financial literacy, ensuring that everyone has access to the knowledge they need to make informed financial decisions. Whether through his books, seminars, or philanthropic efforts, Karl's goal is to equip individuals with the tools to achieve financial independence and security.

Karl's work has transformed the financial landscape for thousands, with readers praising his ability to make the complex world of finance accessible. His seminars have empowered attendees to gain control over their financial future, with many citing his advice as life-changing. Karl's influence stretches globally, with his principles resonating in diverse cultures and economic environments across Europe, Asia, and beyond.

We'd Love Your Feedback

We'd love to hear what you think about this book – just scan in the QR code and fill in the form online, to let us know your feedback.

Thank you!

Sponsored by Hartey Wealth Management

Hartey Wealth Management is a trusted financial planning and wealth management firm, committed to helping individuals and businesses achieve their financial goals. With years of expertise in investment strategies, retirement planning, and estate management, Hartey Wealth Management provides tailored solutions to meet the unique needs of each client. Their team of highly qualified advisers is dedicated to delivering personalised financial advice with a focus on integrity, transparency, and long-term growth.

Contact Hartey Wealth Management:

- Phone: 0808 168 5866

- Email: info@harteywm.co.uk

- Website: www.harteywm.co.uk

Karl and Tristan Hartey

Other Books By Karl Hartey

Financial Education Books for Teenagers and Young Adults:

1.	Smart Money – A teen's guide to understanding and mastering finances

2.	Smart Investments

3.	Smart Insurance

4.	Smart Legal

5.	Smart Business

6.	Smart Retirement

All You Need to Know About Money Series:

1. Retirement

2. Inheritance Tax & Estate Planning

3. Protection

4. Investing

5. Securing Your Family's Financial Future

6. Divorce & Financial Settlements

7. Trusts

8. Long-Term Care

Gumball 3000 Books:

1. 3000 Miles: Our First Gumball Rally

2. Gumball 3000: Miami to Ibiza

3. Gumball 3000: Dublin to Bucharest

4. Gumball 3000: Riga to Mykonos

Other Works:

1. How to Survive the Sharks

2. Educate My Money

Mollie and Tobie Series for Children:

1.   Mollie and Tobie Cornish Tails

2.   Mollie and Tobie Cornish Tails 2

3.   Mollie and Tobie Cornish Tails 3

4.   Mollie and Tobie Greek Tails

5.   Mollie and Tobie Shropshire Tails

Mollie and Tobie Series for Teenagers and Young Adults:

1.   Mollie and Tobie and the Haunted Hall

2.   Mollie and Tobie: The Mystery of the Underground Maze

3.   Mollie and Tobie: The Secret of the Ancient Forest

4.   Mollie and Tobie: The Time Keeper's Legacy

5.   Mollie and Tobie: The Lost City Beneath the Waves

6.   Mollie and Tobie: The Galactic Guardians

7.   Mollie and Tobie: The Clockmaker's Labyrinth

8.   Mollie and Tobie: The Cursed Crown

Printed in Great Britain
by Amazon

50882735R10093